P9-DGZ-493

Because I Loved You

A Birthmother's View of Open Adoption

By
Patricia Dischler

Goblin Fern Press
Madison, Wisconsin

Copyright © 2006 by Patricia Dischler

All rights reserved. No part of this publication may be reproduced or transmitted in any form or by any means, electronic or mechanical, including photocopy, recording or any information storage or retrieval system, except for brief quotations in printed reviews, without prior written permission from the publisher.

Published by
Goblin Fern Press
Madison, Wisconsin
www.goblinfernpress.com
Toll-free: 888-670-BOOK (2665)

Goblin Fern Press books may be purchased in bulk for education, business, fundraising, or sales promotional use. For information, please contact the publisher.

Cataloging-In-Publication Data:
    Dischler, Patricia A.
      Because I loved you : a birthmother's view of open adoption / by Patricia Dischler.
        p. ; cm.

    ISBN-13: 978-1-5959804-2-7
    ISBN-10: 1-59598-042-3
    Includes bibliographical references.

    1. Birthmothers--United States--Biography. 2. Open adoption--United States. 3. Adoption--United States--Psychological aspects. 4. Adopted children--Family relationships. 5. Adoptive parents--Family relationships. 6. Mothers and sons. I. Title.

    HV874.82.D57 B43 2006
    362.82/98/092   2006924351

Cover photograph by Siebe Studio, Dubuque, Iowa,
    (www.siebestudio.com)

Editor: Beth Wallace

Printed in the United States.
10 9 8 7 6 5 4 3 2 1

To Joe,
because this is our story.

To Steve,
who knew we should share it.

TABLE OF CONTENTS

ACKNOWLEDGEMENTS

This book is not only an evolving story but an evolving project as well. The story came first. For this, I would like to thank Nancy Kinley, the adoption counselor who took a stand for honesty and trust and facilitated our open adoption arrangement. I want to thank Jerry and Kathy Temeyer for their years of trust, respect, and understanding. Without them, the story would not exist. I want to thank my family, for supporting me my entire life—even when my choices made their lives difficult. Mom and Dad, I could have never done this without you. I want to thank the doctors and nurses who were so kind to me; I never had the opportunity to show them my gratitude. I want to thank my children, Rachel and Amanda, for reminding me why I need to be strong. I want to thank all those who were a part of this story—whether they feel their part was negative or positive. Because they have allowed me to share it, others will learn from it. And I thank Joe, who always understood the story, even before it was put to words.

Where the story ended, the project began. First, I would like to thank all of my teachers and advisors who supported me in writing about this topic as a Human Issues study for Edgewood College. Special thanks to David Young, who was the first to read it and deem it worthy of print. His praise gave me the confidence to take it further. I need to thank my husband, Steve, who knew before it was even a project that my story was one that needed to be told. I needed the push to get it started, and, as always, he was the one to give me what I needed.

I want to thank Adam Pertman for taking the time to guide me and advise me throughout this venture. His support gave me the determination to see it through. Thank you to Kathleen Silber, who also offered her support in the early stages of the book. I will be forever grateful. Thank you to Carrie Pederman, who was the first to give me a chance to share my story with a group of adoptive parents. That experience gave me the knowledge and understanding I needed to create a book that would make a difference in how birthmothers are viewed.

Thank you to my agent, Jodie Rhodes, who never doubted it should be published, and to Kira Henschel, the publisher, who agreed. Thank you to my friend, Wes Siebe, the only person I could trust to create the book cover photo, and who, as always, created something beautiful.

Finally, I want to thank Beth Wallace, my amazing editor, who once again took my story and shaped it into a book I am proud of. Her guidance and excitement during this project have been invaluable to me, and I truly believe that together we have done our part to bring a little more peace into this world.

FOREWORD

The veil of secrecy has been lifted from adoption. The result is an adoption experience that is healthier and more positive for all parties. In place of closed adoption, which was surrounded by secrecy and shame, there is openness, honesty, and communication. Today the vast majority of domestic infant adoptions are open ones. In open adoption birthparents and adoptive parents exchange full identifying information and have direct access to ongoing contact over the years. The type and frequency of contact varies in each situation, but it is typical for birthparents and adoptive parents to visit once or twice a year (and sometimes more frequently) and to communicate by phone and email between visits. The relationship is similar to that of extended family members. In fact, the birthparents and adoptive parents are related to each other through the adopted child. This reality is the essence of open adoption.

The evolution from closed adoption to semi-open adoption to fully open adoption was a difficult one for the adoption profession and for society in general because many myths and fears surrounded the field of adoption. While the practice of adoption has changed, many of the myths and stereotypes remain in society today. As one of the pioneers of the practice of open adoption, I have seen first hand the benefits of open adoption. As a result, I encourage everyone to move past the myths and fears and to open their hearts to open adoption.

Because I Loved You: A Birthmother's View of Open Adoption tells the story of a semi-open adoption that evolved to a fully open adoption. It also dispels many of the myths. It shows the pain and struggles that are inherent in the decision to place a child for adoption, as well as the positive effects of openness. This book provides help and hope to women considering the option of adoption. Patricia's story of her pregnancy and decision making in the 1980s (in the era of closed adoption) is poignant and compelling.

Patricia was not offered a fully open adoption when she placed her son for adoption. Today's birthparents can maintain an ongoing relationship with the child and his parents from the beginning. As a result, they will not experience some of the pain Pat describes in her book. However, in spite of the difficulties and unknowns that Patricia struggled with in the early years of the adoption of her son, she is a strong advocate for adoption. In each chapter Patricia provides advice and encouragement to birthparents, in addition to relating her personal story. This book will also help adoptive parents, adoptees, and adoption professionals gain a better understanding of the birthparent experience. Through Patricia's personal story, the reader will clearly see the benefits of open adoption for all parties.

While the focus of this book is on the birthparent experience, the reader will also see how the adopted child benefits from openness. The child in an open adoption grows up with communication and honesty. He also knows firsthand that his birthmother placed him in love and still loves him. As a result, the primary beneficiary of open adoption is the child.

Because I Loved You: A Birthmother's View of Open Adoption provides an opportunity for a birthmother's positive story of adoption to be shared and for birthparents and others to gain understanding and hope from this experience.

Kathleen Silber, MSW, ACSW
Co-author of *Dear Birthmother*
and *Children of Open Adoption*

INTRODUCTION

In 1984, I was twenty years old and not married when I became pregnant. I had to tell my family, my friends. Then I had to face the hardest decision of my life. You may be in this same place. Or maybe someone in your family is. It's not a fun place to be. It feels like the end of the world—but it's not.

I chose open adoption for my son because I loved him. It was the best option for my son and for me. I know it was the right thing to do because he is an adult now and I can see how his life and mine have evolved. I know the happy ending. I also know that when you are at this crossroads, happy endings seem impossible.

Adoption has had a bad history. Many stories about adoption are filled with pain and regret. This is because, in the past, women and girls who were unexpectedly pregnant often had no choices. Today you do have choices. Open adoption allows you to know your child is okay. Open adoption provides a line of communication that benefits everyone: birthmothers, adoptive parents, and adoptees.

In this book I explore the full process of adoption: beginning before those fateful words "you're pregnant" are even heard, through the decision-making process, the birth, letting go, and the many years afterward, as the child grows and relationships change. First, each chapter looks at the research, learning from mistakes of the past and giving direction for a successful future. Second, I share in each chapter a portion of my personal story of adoption. It is my hope that the combination will give insight to those trying to understand the thoughts and emotions of a girl or woman going through this process. To those of you facing this decision, I try to offer hope for your future. Adoption can be an amazing experience, filled with love and respect. I know how hard it is to step into the unknown. I hope that by sharing my story with you it won't seem so scary. You can even skip the first part of each chapter and just read the story first—I wrote it for you. You can find the story in each chapter easily by looking at the top of the page and because each page is marked with a floral vine pattern around the number at the bottom of the page.

As my story unfolds in the following chapters, respect, understanding, and love will emerge as the themes. I cannot say that everyone who chooses open adoption will have the same story. This is my story. However, when the elements of respect, understanding, and love are made a fundamental part of the open adoption process, as they were in my experience, success for all involved is inevitable.

If you are facing the choice of adoption for your child, reading this story of success can give you the strength to move forward. Recognizing your commonalities with other birthmothers, like me, as well as your differences, will help you to form your own destiny—and that of your child. In this book, I refer to my unplanned pregnancy as a "mistake." However, I recognize that there are those of you whose pregnancy is the result of failed birth control or even rape. Women find themselves unexpectedly pregnant for many different reasons, but the process of being pregnant and making the best decision for themselves and their babies has similarities for all women. You are an individual, and you deserve to make a personal choice for you and your child. Even though our journeys may be different, I hope that sharing mine will offer you assistance in finding your path as well.

If you are an adoptive parent, this book will help you understand the love and strength it takes for a birthmother to trust you with her child, and help you take those first steps of trust also. Even if you have no contact with the birthmother (such as with foreign adoptions), understanding her point of view will help you in talking with your child about the love that made you a family. For adoptees, this book may help you fully understand the loving choice your mother made for you, and her own sacrifice to do that. For counselors, family members, and all who support a girl or woman through this decision and the years after, this book can guide you in your mission and strengthen you as you see just how deep your influence can be on the outcome of the story.

When my son graduated from high school, I said to his parents, "If I had only known then how it would turn out, it would have been easier." There were many difficult times when doubts seeped in. If I had known how it would end, I would have had more strength to get through it. I offer my story to all of you so you can let go of your doubts, trust in your heart, and make it through the journey ahead of you.

Patricia Dischler

Chapter One

DEFINING MOMENTS

This book is about being pregnant when you hadn't planned to be and about making a decision to keep your baby or place your baby with an adoptive family. This is one of the hardest decisions you will ever make in your life, and there is no single right decision for every woman or girl who faces an unplanned pregnancy. This book will help you understand what the possibilities are for you and for your baby, think through your options carefully, get the support that you need while you are deciding, and make the decision that is right for you, the one that you will not regret.

I want you to understand that while I will be pointing out the benefits of open adoption, and sharing my story of open adoption and how it was successful for everyone, I am not trying to talk you into it or say it will be right for you. It was my choice. It was right for me. I want you to see the benefits of open adoption because I know there is no other book out there right now that will tell you straight up what the next eighteen years could be like if you choose it. Some of the stories you will hear about adoption are scary, but they reflect old practices of closed adoptions before society and counselors knew there was a better way. I want to share my story with you to show you how far adoption has come. The options now are even more positive than what I had, which means you have an even better chance at a bright and happy future. Follow your heart but use your head, and you will find your decision, whether it is to keep your baby or place her for adoption.

Adoption, in any context of the word, conveys change. A change of parents, a change of rules, a change of opinions. In this chapter we will look at the changes over the last twenty years in the field of adoption and at the factors that still await necessary changes. We will also look at how adoption changes the lives of birthmothers. In order to learn from our past and make better decisions for the future, we will explore these topics:

- The history of the changes in domestic adoption;

- The current practices of open adoption;

- False perceptions as well as truths about birthmothers;

- The impact of people's attitudes about unplanned pregnancies and adoption.

For girls and women who are facing a decision about adoption, this chapter will help you understand why your story can be different from the stories you have heard before. For counselors, families, and friends of these girls and women, this chapter will give you a clearer picture of who they are and how important your actions and attitudes will be in their lives. This chapter illustrates for everyone that a birthmother is an individual whose life, while changed by adoption, should never be defined by it.

Adoption in the United States

After years of pain and regret, adoption in America is finally finding its happy ending. Like a large wave at sea that slowly but surely makes it way to shore, open adoption began with a small group of women and their counselors in the 1980s who had the independence and strength to demand change. This wave gathered strength over time and has now crashed down with such force on the shore that the landscape of America will forever be changed.

Changes in the American adoption system over the last twenty years have been slow in coming, and they are not yet complete. For decades adoption was buried in myths, and the choices were limited, and even almost nonexistent. Closed adoptions (where the child is relinquished and has no further contact with the birthmother) were the standard, leaving a wake of regret and pain.

Secrecy was the main cause for the pain that birthmothers of earlier years endured. The secret that they were pregnant left them isolated and lonely; the secret about what happened to their baby left them desperately worried and regretful. Secrecy was used by adoptive parents to avoid pain and worry, but in the end for many families the secrets were difficult to keep up and caused more severe pain than what families were trying to avoid. Secrecy for adoptees became a source of broken trust and harmed relationships not only with their adoptive parents but with their birthmothers as well.

In *Adoptions Today: Questions and Controversies* author Ann E. Weiss discusses the benefits of open adoption:

> For adoptees, there is no secrecy, so there is no need for lies or romantic tales, no playing "As If." Birthparents who choose open adoption feel less of a sense of loss than parents who have to accept never seeing their child again. Just as important, they get to help choose the adoptive family. . . . It leaves a birthmother feeling more secure about the home in which her child is being raised. The adoptive parents benefit from living without the burden of lies and evasions.

From Weiss's perspective, doing away with the secrecy surrounding closed adoptions benefits everyone involved in the adoption.

A relationship of honesty and communication between birthmothers and adoptive families eliminates or minimizes much of the pain and worry for all parties. This does not preclude pain for the birthmother in particular—relinquishing a child under the best of circumstances is still a painful act. But it does leave fewer issues of concern. It creates a communication link between parties, which will make addressing any remaining issues possible.

Adam Pertman summarizes it well:

> The bottom line, though, is that greater openness for adoptees means an upbringing rooted in self-knowledge and truth rather than equivocation or deception; for birth parents, it helps diminish angst and permits grieving, and therefore increases their comfort levels with their decisions; and for adoptive parents, it eases personal insecurities while establishing a steady stream of information for their children and for making critical parenting decisions (based, for example, on the birth family's medical history).

As one of the birthmothers who belonged to that group of mavericks who stood up and fought the limitations of closed adoption and insisted on the honesty and respect that open adoption offered, I am delighted to know that over 90 percent of domestic infant adoptions in the United States today are open adoptions.

The Current Practices of Open Adoption

The basic idea behind open adoption is to create a connection between adoptive families and birth families. A line of communication is established. This communication in adoption varies from "semi-open," in which letters and/or photos are exchanged on a yearly basis, to "fully open," in which the birthmother is welcomed into the home of the adoptive family and ongoing communication occurs. Most often the communication arrangement is somewhere in the middle. The parties may have direct access to each other: names, addresses, phone numbers. Or they may exchange their information through a third party, usually the adoption agency.

An open adoption arrangement is also flexible, changing according to the needs of the child as he grows older. While letters and photos may be sufficient while the child is young, she may request a personal visit as she grows older and has more questions. Open adoption allows all members of the adoption "triad" (birthmothers, adoptive parents, and adoptees) to voice their changing needs. The basis of respect between all members paths the way for these needs to be met.

Open adoption minimizes the pain (although nothing can remove it completely) and problems that were associated with closed adoptions. Of families who participated in open adoptions, according to Harriet Gross, "90% are very satisfied with the adoption and 95% definitely would do this adoption again."

Birthmothers

The pressures of society and its judgments of a young mother's decision reach into every aspect of her life. Often societal pressure preempts a birthmother's decision, many times without her awareness. In *Waiting to Forget,* birthmother Margaret Moorman states, "It is my conviction that in most cases it is the prevailing moral climate that makes real reproductive choice possible or impossible for a pregnant girl or woman." In the past, the outcome of societal judgment of birthmothers was a generation who chose closed adoption and accepted its veils of secrecy. At the time, it was fully believed that this decision would create the least amount of pain for all those involved and provide a future for both mother and child unaffected by circumstances of the event. As registries expand nationwide for both birthmothers and adoptees searching for each other, it becomes increasingly clear that these parties were anything *but* unaffected.

There was no conscious intention to take away choices from these mothers, and certainly no one purposefully sent these women and children into a future filled with pain and regret. Decisions in favor of closed adoption were made by a society filled with good intentions based upon bad assumptions. The information used to make these choices was false. Myths about birthmothers and about the needs of adoptive children affected decisions about adoption. It would be decades before researchers would be successful in changing these views. Specifically, the decision that closed adoption was best for everyone rested on these myths: that birthmothers choose adoption because they did not care for their child; that no contact would make it easier for the birthmother to forget; that secrecy would protect the child from being judged and keep the birthmother from changing her mind; and finally, that the child would have no desire to know his or her birthparents.

The base of this problem lies in society and sometimes even with researchers who try to place birthmothers in a neat little box where they can be labeled.

It's logical that if birthmothers are all the same, then there should be one "right answer" to the problem we face. Yet these women and girls are not all the same. You cannot put them in a box. And so the best solution for one birthmother is likely to be different from the solution for another.

As with any identity label, that of "birthmother" creates an image for those who hear it. Most often, the image is one of a girl whose morals are lacking, whose financial status is poor, and who has little or no family support in her life. The general public tends to have this picture in their mind as a result of a general urge to categorize. It is always much easier to have a commonly agreed upon definition for a term than to explore its varied complexities. This is true of almost everything in our world: an apple is in the fruit aisle right along with the papaya, even though they grew in very different climates and took very different journeys to reach that same place.

While I'm pretty sure the apple and papaya couldn't care less if you knew about their life before the fateful day you met them while shopping, I am certain that every birthmother you meet would prefer you did not form an opinion about who she is based on one event in her life, however meaningful.

Adam Pertman found this tendency to compartmentalize birthmothers equally troubling: "The lingering cultural stereotype of birthmothers as uncaring or ignorant young teens who choose adoption to crassly jettison a nettlesome problem is unmitigated and corrosive nonsense."

Yes, placing a child for adoption is a defining moment for a woman; it forever changes the path of her life. But it does not negate the fact that she had a "before," that she is a person whose life began years before hearing the fateful words "you're pregnant," and that the experiences of that life "before" did as much to shape who she is as her choice for adoption did.

Too often birthmother stories begin with the pregnancy and end nine months later with relinquishment. In order to truly understand the choices of these women, it's important to understand their past. Their experiences of family, children, love and marriage, sex and conception, not only contribute to the choices that led to the pregnancy but also lay a foundation for their journey through the options they then face.

As birthmothers, our ages range from young teenagers to adults. Our financial statuses are as varied as the water levels in the Mississippi. We have families who love us, who ignore us, and who do not exist at all. We are intelligent; we are troubled. We are strong and independent; we are lost and frightened. We are angry; we are elated. We are confused; we are informed. We are scared; we are determined. We are as multifaceted and individual as glistening snowflakes, with the same fragility and the same potential to be strengthened as we join others.

Our commonalties go no further than our journey through a complicated decision. We each approach the crossroads of adoption from a different path, and we will each forge our own new path leading from it. Society may continue to excavate roads to and from that fundamental choice of whether to keep or to relinquish our babies, paving them, presenting them as the smoothest, softest path to follow. But the road to truth is never smooth. The only answer is to gather the tools of knowledge and information and to build a new path—for each woman to build the right path for herself and for her child.

When I first found out about my pregnancy, I was shocked. I didn't fit the societal image of "birthmother," so how could it be true? What I now know is that there is no mold. A body doesn't get pregnant because of lack of money or family or even because of poor morals. Unplanned pregnancies happen either because a woman is misinformed or because she has made a choice to ignore the information and take a chance. Even when informed and making good choices pregnancies can happen. Birth control fails. Rape occurs.

In the same way that misconceptions about pregnant women lead to poor choices by society, the misconceptions these women and girls hold about sex and conception often lead to the pregnancy in the first place. This was the case with me. When I was doing research for my book, I was relieved to find out I was not alone. In *I'm Pregnant, Now What Do I Do?* the authors write, "There are a lot of misconceptions among teens about how to prevent a pregnancy. If this happens to you, there's no reason to feel stupid. Other teens have similar misconceptions and become pregnant when they don't want to." They gave a list of common misconceptions, and I was shocked: at age twenty I had believed almost all of the items on the list!

I was split between feeling comforted that I wasn't the only one and feeling even more stupid because I wasn't a "teen" at the time and yet believed so many things that were false. But I didn't have anyone (other than my boyfriend) to fill me in. All of my girlfriends were virgins, and my mom got so nervous just discussing my period that I was afraid she'd self-combust if I mentioned sex.

But as I did more research and read more about how so many young women do not know all the details of reproduction, it felt good to know I wasn't alone. For the first time in years I began to forgive myself and move past feeling stupid to understand that I had simply been uninformed. Birthmothers need to know that they are not alone in having misconceptions or in having those misconceptions lead to an unexpected pregnancy. Knowledge is powerful—with it you can make choices you can stand by. Without good information, often the choices are made for you.

The Impact of Attitude

We've come a long way as a society. A dialogue between those in the adoption triad and general society has begun, and we are learning from each other and respecting the intense emotions that this issue can evoke. But there is still much work to be done.

When a girl or woman tells others of an unplanned pregnancy, the most common response is: "What are you going to do now?" While it is a question that must be explored and answered, it is a disservice to the birthmother—and to her child—to expect an answer without giving her the opportunity to gather knowledge about herself and her options. It is more than just looking at the options ahead that is necessary—it is also essential to look back. Understanding her prior experiences and the knowledge she has gained from these experiences is important in making a good decision.

Supporting girls and women as they find their own destinies and that of their children can be as simple as telling them they can do it. Offer clear, accurate, unbiased information, and create the support network necessary to facilitate productive decision making. Whether you meet a woman facing these decisions formally as a professional, encounter her casually through a friend or chance meeting, or find her in the middle of your own family or friendship circle, it's important to remember that how you treat her will affect her decision—and the life of a child.

Remember that "what to do now" is an extremely personal decision. The answers are unique to each woman or girl. Celebrate this individuality by helping the girl see her personal strengths, face her weaknesses, and move forward with confidence. Rather than trying to help her find an answer, help her to find her self-confidence. If her pregnancy was the result of being misinformed, or making a bad choice, offer comments like these:

♦ You are strong and smart; you are capable of making the right decision for you.

♦ You've made a mistake, but you are a good person and you will find a way to fix it.

♦ Being misinformed is not the same as being stupid. You just need more information. Let me help you get it.

♦ I trust in you to do what is right for you and your baby.

♦ One bad decision does not define who you are. We all make mistakes. Now is your time to learn all you can and make an informed choice.

♦ I can help you to explore your choices, but I believe in you and when you have all the information you will know what to do.

Additionally, if the pregnancy occurred due to failed birth control or rape, offer her support in knowing she did nothing wrong but that she can control what happens next.

My story illustrates this optimal support system and how it can work. Each person who came into my life, showed me love, and supported my independence and decision-making capabilities—both before and after I discovered that I was pregnant—contributed to the happy ending.

In this chapter I share my personal story to illustrate some of the details of the "before" that influenced my "after." I was one of the lucky ones—I had many positive influences in my life. I recognize now how that fact helped me to make the best decision for my son and for me. Not every person I encountered offered a positive response. In fact, in the first few months after I discovered I was pregnant, many people were shocked, negative, or even hurtful. However, my core support system—my parents, close friends, and counselor—was supportive and positive. This gave me the strength to deal with the negative reactions. Additionally, I had been supported in my decision-making abilities throughout my life, creating a basis from which to face these new obstacles.

It is my hope that by reading my story, you will see how your actions can influence a woman or girl not just during the time she faces a decision about a pregnancy but, as the self-confidence you help to create helps her overcome obstacles, throughout the rest of her life. For birthmothers, I share my story as a sign of respect. You are as individual as I am. We all have a story to tell, and we all deserve the respect of having someone listen to it. I hope that by reading mine, you will gain the strength to tell yours someday. I hope to empower you through your decision-making process. Remember that while your life is now changed forever by the fact that you will have a child, it does not define you. You have had a life up until now, you will have a life after your pregnancy, and both of them count. The experiences of your past will guide you today and in the future. You are in charge of your life. You are also now responsible for the life of a child. Use what you already know, and learn what you need to know, and you will find your way to the decisions that will help you—and your child—find your own happy endings.

MY STORY BEGINS...

Up until 1984 my life was pretty simple—in fact, some would say it was perfect. I had an incredibly close family. Growing up on a beautiful farm surrounded by horses, nature, and love left my heart so full of wonderful memories that my friends listen to the stories with disbelief. At twenty years old I had yet to meet someone whose childhood topped my own. Dubuque, Iowa, was a beautiful place to grow up in the 60s and 70s. One of the few places in Iowa that isn't flat, Dubuque is blessed by the bluffs and valleys formed by the mighty Mississippi River. My memories of childhood are all happy: sledding down the bluffs with my three younger sisters, Sue, Karen, and Jane; camping in the fields with my cousins; making pickles with Mom and throwing hay bales with Dad. What I didn't realize until later was that everyone's life has conflict and sadness in it somewhere. Instead of peppering my life throughout, my trials were just waiting to begin, and in 1984, when I was twenty, the first cracks in my perfect life appeared.

"Dropping the ball" on New Year's usually refers to Dick Clark's New Year's Rockin' Eve Show and the ball of light that descends from a tower in New York, symbolizing the passing of one year and the start of a new one. For me, "dropping the ball" meant my high school sweetheart, my first love, telling me he had been cheating on me for most of our four-year relationship and he was now breaking up with me so he could openly date his current sidekick. He told me at my New Year's party, and as I listened, I looked into the living room and saw my friends toasting the New Year, singing and dancing—celebrating.

I was devastated. Everything started to spiral down as fast as that glistening ball on Dick Clark's show. Eric was my soul mate. I had been sure of it for over four years now, and I fully expected to receive a marriage proposal at any moment. I was completely thrown off my rocker without him.

However, as a horse rider, I knew the first rule was that when the horse bucked you off, you got up and got back on. Your butt might hurt, but you kept going. Eric might have bruised my heart, but I wasn't about to stop living because of it. My best friend, Lori, helped me keep my balance, and I got back on that horse and rode. Actually, it was a motorcycle, my only transportation in those days.

To her parents' dismay, I took Lori on long rides almost every afternoon, unless it snowed hard—then we went skiing. I volunteered to teach Sunday School at my church and even trekked the three miles on cross country skis to get there one Sunday after a big snowstorm.

My printing company was off to a running start, keeping me busy, and by spring I moved from my dinky apartment and rented a nice house. My family was as tight as ever, talking on the phone every day and seeing each other often. My sister Sue, at eighteen, had just left home to join the Navy, but seventeen-year-old Karen and thirteen-year-old Jane were still in school and involved in so many activities we always had a game or other event to attend together. As a former competitive motorcycle racer, my dad secretly relished the idea that I had followed in his footsteps and was always available to fix my bike. I was excited about my life moving into adulthood, and I enjoyed the balance we had found between my new independence and still being one of my parents' kids.

I met Brad in February, and we quickly became good buddies. We started to spend a lot of time together talking, riding our motorcycles, and camping with other friends. In May, we took an all-night motorcycle ride, ending up on the shore of the Mississippi. As the sun rose, with one short, sweet, kiss my entire future began to change.

We began to date, having wonderful adventures and enjoying every ounce of summer. One evening, after a glorious midnight motorcycle ride through flooded streets after a storm, we went to his apartment, shared a six-pack of beer, and shared his bed.

I won't make excuses by blaming the alcohol. It was a bad choice. I cared a lot for Brad, but even at the time I knew it was a bad choice. I had slept with someone who was not the man I thought I was meant to spend the rest

17

of my life with. By crossing the line from a great friendship to an intimate relationship, I had also lost a good friend.

Realizing my mistake hit me so hard that I got up, got dressed, and was out the door before Brad knew what was happening. I drove my motorcycle as best I could while shaking uncontrollably, and when I got home, took the longest, hottest shower of my life. Three days later I told Brad I couldn't see him anymore. He was a great friend, and I cared about him a lot. It hurt to hurt him, but I was so embarrassed by my mistake of sleeping with him that I couldn't bring myself to talk to him about it.

My mom and I had never discussed sex. The closest we came was when I was in sixth grade, after we had seen a sex education film at school. She said, "Do you have any questions?" I quickly answered, "No," and ran outside to ride my horse and to try to figure out on my own how Sammy Sperm got over to Edna Egg (this portion of the film seemed to have been deleted). I came to the conclusion that you must have to drink the guy's pee. *Gross,* I thought. *Looks like I'll never have kids.* Most of what I knew about sex when I was twenty I had learned from the guys I had dated, and trust me, girls—you shouldn't believe a word they say. So what I didn't know until two months after I slept with Brad was that you could get pregnant while you have your period.

The next few weeks I buried myself in work. My long hours drove my housemate crazy, so in July, Lori and I decided to move into an apartment together. Even Eric

and I began talking and working things out. Then I began to feel nauseated at work.

I had pulled an all-nighter in order to finish a big project we did for the Dubuque Tourism Society. I started feeling tired and nauseated the next day, so I cut out early and went home to bed. The next morning I didn't feel much better, but since I was sure it was due to lack of sleep and stress, I dragged myself to work, promising to make it a short day and get to bed early. I spent most of the day in the bathroom. A woman from another business in the building came into the bathroom during one particularly bad stretch and asked if I was okay. I told her I'd been working too much, and she said she had morning sickness so bad with her first child that she had to quit work. I stared at her in disbelief and said I was not pregnant—it was just the flu. She apologized and left quickly.

I went back to my light table and stared at the work piled on it, thinking, *What, is she crazy? How could she think I was pregnant? That's ridiculous. I just had my period a couple of weeks ago.* Then I looked up at the calendar hanging next to my desk. I looked back a few days, then weeks, for the familiar "Aunt Flow" notation. It wasn't there. I looked back further but couldn't find the code word written until I had gone back two months, one day before "Meet Brad on bike at park." *No,* I thought, *I just forgot to write it down. I remember that I bled after breaking up with Brad.* I ran to the bathroom as another wave of nausea hit.

The next few days I was in such a daze, the memories are like an old silent movie, flickering in my mind in quick, short, disconnected scenes. Telling Lori I'd been sick. Lori reminding me that I had bled because I had had a urinary tract infection. Going to Planned Parenthood. Waiting for the test result. Overwhelming embarrassment in finding out you certainly can get pregnant during your period. Getting the test result. Feeling my world slip away. The doctor telling me I was two months along. Telling Lori. Accepting the horror that this event would bring an abrupt halt to any reconciliation with Eric. All of this peppered with clips of throwing up and hours of crying uncontrollably. The downward spiral of events and emotions once again reminded me of that fateful globe of light descending on New Year's Eve.

Then the fast forward pace of my memory comes to an abrupt halt, the moment eclipsing any sense of time. I was sitting in my parents' living room on the couch. My mom was on the bench for our old upright piano, a place I had spent thousands of happy hours having sing-alongs with my family. Dad was sitting stiffly on the orange recliner next to the piano, and they were waiting for me to speak.

"Mom, Dad, I'm pregnant." The words almost choked me. My head fell; my shoulders sank. It had taken every ounce of strength I had just to say those words. I thought it was the hardest thing I would ever have to do. I was dead wrong.

I raised my head to stare across the room, through the window covered with shelving and plants out into the

barnyard. The horses were out there. I wished so badly that I were too. Life was always uncomplicated when I sat on Dusty or rode Brandy through the clover.

My dad's abrupt cough snapped me back to the room, back to face what I was sure would be nothing short of a death sentence. I looked at my mom. I don't think she had taken a breath since I issued my statement. The pain and disbelief in her eyes gripped my heart so tight that I was sure in the next moment my death would come in the form of a heart attack. No such luck. In a surprisingly calm voice my dad asked, "Who?"

"Brad."

"I figured you were foolin' around, but I also figured you were smart enough to use protection." Dad sat tall and straight with his hands lying flat on the arms of the orange recliner. His voice was rising now, and I braced myself for the full explosion.

"But Dad, we . . . I mean, I. . . ." I fidgeted on the couch, hiding my hands under my bottom.

"None of it really matters now, does it?" said Mom. Dad snapped a look at her. Another pang of guilt hit my heart—that look was meant for me. But we all knew the time for should have's, would have's, could have's was a lifetime ago. The questions of right and wrong would be answered, but not right now. Now there was only one question.

In barely more than a whisper, her dark eyes pooling with tears, my mom asked, "What are you going to do?"

The words hung thick in the air, choking any answer I might have had—not that I had one. So far I had only

had time to think about how my parents would murder me at this point. It seemed futile to look past the explosion. I stared at my dad, waiting in a trance for him to pounce and for this to be over. I was prepared for the anger. I was not prepared for what did happen.

Dad leaned towards me, my eyes locked with his. His steel blue eyes were clouded with pain and worry. It broke my heart in two. *This is worse than death,* I thought. *I've killed my father's spirit.* Although there was sadness in his eyes, he did not tear up. He simply said, "We'll get through this together. Thank you for telling us." That was it. I broke down in sobs that shook my entire body. I couldn't breathe; I couldn't think—all I could do was cry. I don't know what my parents did during this time; I was too absorbed in the painful realities that were finally sinking in. Telling my parents was not the hardest thing I've ever had to do. No, there were things ahead that would be much worse, and for the first time I realized this.

Slowly, my parents went over the painful options. Would we get married? No. I had witnessed an uncle get married for this reason, only to watch him divorce four years later. Abortion? Fearfully my parents asked where I stood. My response gave them their first breath of relief. Not an option, I replied. This was a child, a gift from God. I could never kill it because I was too selfish to accept the responsibility. Adoption? I was just accepting the idea that I was having a baby. I wasn't ready yet to let it go. Keep it? My first choice, I told them.

Dad was quiet. Mom pointed out the many problems with that choice. I owned a printing company; where would the baby be when I worked? "I'll bring it with," I answered.

"Don't you think your baby deserves what you had? A family, together; a home; a mother to raise him?" Mom was poised on the edge of the bench. Dad hadn't moved.

I wasn't ready to answer these questions. At the time all I could think of was that I was going to have a baby. I could picture holding him—not handing him over to a stranger. It would hurt me too much. After a short debate I agreed to explore my options in more detail before deciding. We'd been through enough for one day. Emotionally drained, I hugged each of them, saying "I'm sorry," between sobs. Mom went to the kitchen to start supper.

I am the same age now that my mother was then. Perhaps that is why I feel compelled to revisit those places in my heart and memory. I now can attempt to see and understand more by looking through her eyes. I have two daughters now. Just thinking of the past, considering a similar event in my own daughters' lives, tears at my heart and clenches my stomach. I know now that this is how Mom felt. This fear is what kept her from forming words in those first moments.

Fear affects people in many different ways. I had a writing teacher in college who, after reading a short story I wrote, commented on the father character in the story. At the time he didn't know that the character was in real life my own father. In the story, the character had some tough times but worked through them with honor and

grace, just as my dad always had. My teacher liked the character but thought I should "turn up the heat under him and see what he does." In the months following my announcement I don't think the heat could have been turned up any higher.

While I now understand fear and love were the driving forces behind all my father's actions, at the time all I saw was that I had managed to find my father's boiling point. As we spent time together throughout my pregnancy, Dad would give me jobs to do on the farm like stacking hay or fixing fences. Most of the time it felt like punishment. Work was Dad's favorite form of discipline—and very effective too. (I still remember the time my cousin Debbie and I decided to cover ourselves in mud down at the crick during a family picnic at our house—wearing our good clothes. Dad made us pick up all the sticks in the pasture. Redundant work, but we had plenty of time to think, and I know I *never* got my good clothes dirty again.)

So each time he threw a big job my way during my pregnancy, I dutifully plugged away until it was done, ignoring the nausea or light-headedness. But each time I felt sure that the only reason he gave me the job was to let me know he was mad in the only way he knew how. Denial seemed to be Dad's standard during those days. He never treated me any differently; he never asked about the baby or how I was feeling. If I did talk about it, he'd make some excuse to leave the room. He never verbally expressed his anger, but I could feel it each time he hollered at me to hurry up and unload a wagon of hay.

As promised, the week after telling my parents, I went to see my doctor. Dr. Storm had delivered my sisters and me, had stitched up the cuts I got every summer going barefoot, and had been the first to explain what a menstrual period was. I didn't see why I needed to see him, but Mom insisted. His office was in an old building downtown. There was paneling on the walls and a collection of mismatched office chairs in the waiting room. Old coffee tables held copies of *Highlights* magazine that had been there since I was a kid. A nurse left me to wait in an exam room, and I thought about how Dr. Storm would be delivering a second generation of our family.

Dr. Storm's hair was all white now, but his actions were still swift. His stern blue eyes looked through the too-big frames straight at me. It took less than a second for my smile to fade.

"How do you know you're pregnant?" Dr. Storm snapped.

"I had a test at Planned Parenthood."

"That's a horrible place." He didn't even bother to sit, saying, "Well, let's take a look and see what's going on. The gown is on the table. I'll be back in a minute." He left me sitting there, staring at the gown, wondering what in the world we were going to look at. My stomach was still flat.

A few minutes later he returned with a nurse. I was in my gown, sitting self-consciously on the table and trying to hold it closed behind me. My feet were cold, and I was beginning to feel sick to my stomach.

After some merciless rooting around, he snapped off his cold gloves and told me to get dressed as he left the room. Whatever he had done, it had hurt, and for the first time I worried about my baby. I laid my hand on my stomach and whispered, "It'll be okay." A feeling washed over my body I had never had before. I tingled all over yet felt paralyzed for the moment. It was in that instant that I began to fall in love with my baby. I held my stomach and smiled.

"So, what do your parents think about this?" Dr. Storm burst out as he entered the room again.

"What?" I asked, sitting up tall.

"Your parents," he said. "They must be very disappointed that you'd do something this stupid."

I sat and stared at him. I had always known Dr. Storm was tough, like the time he slapped me because I screamed when he stuck a needle into an inch-deep cut in my arm that bared the bone. Somehow his words hurt more.

"Don't have any answer, do you?" he snapped. "I suppose it's too late to teach you any morals now." He got up and hit my file on the desk, saying, "Come back next month." And he was gone.

I cried all the way home. I knew I would have to face the morality of what I had done. I just never expected it to happen while with my doctor. He was right, of course—that's why I didn't argue with him. But shouldn't he be more concerned about my health and my baby's health? The more I thought about the cruel exam, I began to question if he didn't secretly want my baby to be

harmed—or worse—lost completely. I had to ask the nurse at the front desk some of my questions, because Dr. Storm had said his piece and left. I wasn't even sure what questions to ask so I felt more confused than ever after the visit.

When Mom called that night, I simply said that everything was fine and I had another appointment next month.

Over the next week my morning sickness expanded into the afternoon. Eating saltines in bed before I got up only provided something other than green slime to fill the toilet later. At work I was spending more time in the bathroom than at my drafting table. I was worried that my business partner was going to get upset about it, but he was surprisingly nice to me. I called Dr. Storm's office to set my next appointment, hoping he could offer help but not expecting him to give it to me.

"I'm sorry," the nurse said. "Dr. Storm is retiring. All his patients are being referred to the Medical Circle Clinic. Would you like their number?"

Would I! "Yes, please," I answered, while mentally saying a little prayer of thanks to God. I called and set my appointment for the next week. I was getting pretty sick and didn't want to wait a month.

By the end of the week I couldn't work anymore. I stayed home and battled my stomach. On one day I was so determined to keep something down that I ate one bowl of cereal, threw it up, and ate another, all morning long. By noon I had thrown up an entire box of Honey Nut Cheerios. I haven't been able to stand the sight of

them ever since.

The new clinic was all I had hoped for. It was bright, new, clean, and full of friendly faces. The nurses were kind, and for the first time I didn't feel as if I were being tried and convicted. It felt as if it had been months since I sat nervously waiting for Dr. Storm to enter. Now I waited calmly, thinking clearly of all my questions.

Dr. Whalen walked in. He was tall, much younger than Dr. Storm, and too handsome not to notice.

"Hello, Patty," said Dr. Whalen. "How're you feeling today?" He smiled a kind, warm smile and sat down across from me. "It says here you've had some morning sickness."

"Yes," I answered. "I usually only throw up in the morning, but I feel like I'm going to most of the day, so I'm always in the bathroom."

"That's too bad," he said. I had a flash in my head of Dr. Storm saying, "Serves you right."

"How far along are you?" he asked.

"A little more than two months," I answered.

"Well," he said, "the good news is you should start feeling better in the next couple of weeks. Are you having any problems other than the nausea?"

"No, I'm okay," I said. What a lie.

He gave me a big smile, and I knew he knew better. "Let's do the exam and we can talk more after, okay?"

"Sure," I said. When he left the room, I put my hand on my tummy and said, "Don't worry any more, dear. Dr. Whalen will take good care of you."

During the next few weeks I had to come to terms with the shame and guilt of becoming pregnant. To tell or not to tell became a huge burden. Telling meant facing reactions of shame or pity that I had not settled within my own mind yet. Not telling felt like lying or hiding, both of which I had been taught not to do. I feared the reactions, yet at the same time I yearned for someone to talk to, who would understand how I was feeling. In 1984 in Dubuque I knew I would be facing a lot of old-fashioned views about sex and pregnancy. I had to rely on the understanding and support of my family and close friends to give me the patience to deal with the confusion caused by those who judged me.

In telling Eric I faced the shame that it would not be his baby. He pointed this out as his reasoning for pulling away from me. I realize now how selfish this was of him. We had broken up because he was cheating on me. I was not with him when I slept with Brad. I was not the one who should have felt shame. If he had really cared for me, he might have been able to acknowledge this and be there for me. I remember getting a phone call from Eric's mother begging me to stay out of her son's life. The call confused me because she spoke to me as if I were a bad person, a sinner, a slut—someone with no future, no morals. I'd never thought of myself in those terms before.

I knew that Mom and Dad were trying very hard to keep my pregnancy secret. They were telling no one, and especially not anyone at church. Mom was petrified about how our small-town Catholic church would react.

She was the organist. Dad helped run the pancake breakfast each year. They were both deeply involved, and all their friends were people from our church. For their generation, keeping the baby would not only create a "bastard" but label me a sinner and a slut as well. They couldn't bear the humiliation, and I couldn't bear to be the cause of it. I knew that for the people at my parents' church, seeing me pregnant would be the same as wearing a scarlet letter: they would know I had sinned. At the time, the embarrassment of everyone knowing what sin I had committed was enough for my parents to suggest that I not attend church with them anymore. The idea that I caused my parents to feel shame was enough to bring me to tears.

Thinking about how my parents' friends in the church would react also made me very angry. To be fair, since I didn't go to church, we never actually experienced a negative reaction, but I know my parents had told a few select people and that they were generalizing the reactions of those few to the entire congregation. Still, I didn't believe any of them had the right to judge my parents or me. We weren't the only family dealing with issues that resulted from sin. My parents, and our church, had preached the verse "Let he who has not sinned cast the first stone" to us girls for long enough that we had learned how wrong it was to judge others. So it seemed unfair that my parents feared judgment from a congregation that was taught not to judge. Sometimes I wanted to show up at church and announce that I was pregnant just to dare someone to judge me in front of our priest.

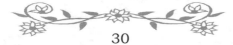

I had always been considered a good kid. Good grades, involved in lots of activities, a good friend, I taught Sunday School at my church and always tried my best at everything I did. I was ambitious and creative and lived each day to the fullest. I still felt like the same person. Did I become someone else without realizing it? It's a question I still wrestle with.

I remember girls in school labeling other girls as sluts. If you were seen hanging on boys in the hall, the girls would spread the rumor that you would be "knocked up" soon. No one ever predicted that about me. Yet here I was. The thing is, the girls who actually were having sex were probably smart enough to go on the pill. I didn't even know it existed until after having my baby. Did the simple fact that I was pregnant make me a slut? I did sleep with someone I was not married to. Was that the definition? It was scary. The only conclusion I was able to come to then is that either I was a good kid who made a bad choice or if I were a slut, then people who are sluts have no idea that they are.

The labels teenagers place on one another seem so insignificant now. Back then, a label was everything. Everyone had one, and you constantly worried about what yours would be. I knew better than to judge a person by a single act. My parents had been very clear on the issue of getting to know a person before forming an opinion based on a stereotype, but this didn't stop me from worrying that others would label me. As an adult, I see how petty it is and how unproductive and hurtful. I under-

stand the complexities of people and situations, and I have the self-confidence to make my way in life without worrying about what others may think. However, in 1984 I was still in the process of learning these facts.

There was one thing Eric's mom had said that I was sure of: I had sinned. But I wouldn't get the opportunity to talk to a priest and put this sin behind me until much later. For now, I had to look forward—not back.

Every time I told someone, the negative reaction knocked me down. It didn't take long before I learned not to tell unless it was necessary. I even avoided Mom and Dad for a while—it was too hard to see their disappointed faces. I was doing all I could to wrap myself in denial. I was tired of hurting, of crying, of feeling hopeless. I started to convince myself everything was going to turn out great.

Despite all the bad things, I was determined to make everything work. I cried less often as time went by, and I even had moments of hope and happiness. I fantasized that someday Eric and I would find a way to get through this and that somehow my dreams of being a family would all come true.

By the end of August there was just one loose end—Brad. I called, and he came over the next day. He drove up to the front of my building and parked. I was sitting on a stone wall that surrounded the stairs to the building. He joined me on the wall, and in one look I knew he already knew. But I still had to form the words, make it real. "I'm pregnant," was all I could say. He looked so sad.

"I figured that's what it was when you called," he said. We sat there a minute in silence. Then he said, "Do you want to get married?"

I was so shocked that at first I just looked at him and blinked. He looked scared to death. It felt like a scene in a movie where the camera pulls away, making people who are still standing next to each other all of a sudden look as if they have moved farther away. He looked so young all of a sudden. I felt so old. "No," I said, shaking my head. "That's not going to solve anything."

"Are you sure?" he asked, "Because I will if you think it's the right thing to do."

I was so impressed. He was sweating, but I don't think it was because of the late summer heat. He couldn't look me in the eyes. "I'm sure," I answered. He let out a sigh and seemed to physically deflate in front of me. He looked tired.

He looked over to the street where my motorcycle was parked. "Are you still driving your bike?" he asked, this time with some real concern in his voice.

"Sure, at least until my belly doesn't fit!" I answered, and laughed. It hadn't occurred to me until that moment that it was probably a bit odd for a pregnant woman to drive a motorcycle. Heck, in a town like Dubuque, it was odd for me to ride it at all, just being a girl.

"Well, if the weather's bad or somethin' and you need a ride, you can call me," he said.

"Thanks," I answered. I hopped down from the wall. I felt good. Everything was going to be fine. I still didn't

know exactly how, but I was sure it was. "Thanks for coming," I said. "I'll call and keep you updated."

"Okay," he said. He gave me an awkward hug, and with a forced smile he nodded, turned, and drove away. It was the last time I ever saw him.

Chapter Two

Individual Pathways

A
fter the initial shock of discovering an unplanned pregnancy, there is a transition period when life is inventoried, choices are explored, and your body changes. Your instincts kick in and tell you one thing, while your support system may be saying something different. Your hormones surge, and your body changes. Along with physical changes, other kinds of change begin to occur in your life. As things shift, your focus may shift. Your plans may change; your decisions may become easier to make—or harder. The changes that occur in these months leading to the birth of your child are filled with emotions, and so they should also be filled with those you most trust to offer support.

This chapter will explore all these changes you may face. It will help you to take inventory of your life, giving you the information you will need to make the best decision for you and your child. For those supporting a girl or woman during this time, this chapter will give you direction for aiding her in this task of facing the realities of her inventory. To accomplish these goals we will discuss the following topics:

- Initial instincts and keeping an open mind.
- Taking inventory of your life and support system.
- Reacting to change in your inventory or instincts.
- Handling the physical and emotional effects of pregnancy.
- Loving your child.

Keeping an Open Mind

Pregnancy brings out a woman's instincts. For many, the instinct to protect at all costs comes first. This may lead to a determination to keep your child. Or it may lead to a determination to place the child with someone you feel is more capable of being a mother. Instinct may tell you that you would be a great mother—and should be. Instinct may tell you that you are too scared or inexperienced to try. It's okay to have any of these instincts. Often instincts can help you to make decisions when the facts are unclear or confusing. What's important to remember is that you should still take the time to collect information and facts. They may confirm what you instinctively know. Or they may contradict it. In the end you will weigh both the facts and your instincts to come to a decision.

When a woman's instincts are telling her that she would be a wonderful mother, caring and loving, it becomes very difficult to accept any circumstances in her life, or changes that occur, that interfere with this instinct. But obstacles should not be ignored. Until you have taken the time to confirm that you have the life inventory necessary to raise a child, or accept that you do not but possibly could find the necessary resources, you should not make any decisions. Taking the time to see what you have to offer a child and what support you have for yourself is not designed to talk you into or out of adoption or any other choice. It is an intellectual journey to put you in a place where you can make a decision without regrets.

Families and counselors should respect the natural instincts of a mother but also help her to face the realities of her life and parenting so she will be clear on what will be needed. She can then determine if she possesses these skills and resources, is able to obtain them, or cannot or does not wish to learn them. This will only be one factor in making a final decision, but it's an important one to explore.

Choosing adoption for your child does not mean you have decided that you would not be a good mother, as you may fear. Adam Pertman reports on the feelings of birthparents: "while they know that physiologically they can become mothers and fathers, they strongly believe they aren't prepared to be parents. The distinction may be subtle, but it's critical." These birthparents understood the difference between being a mother and parenting a child. If you have taken the time to do your inventory and be honest with yourself, you will understand the difference as well.

If you are a young teen mother, the idea of a sweet young baby who would love you unconditionally may sound wonderful at a time in your life when all your relationships are being tested. This idealistic view of motherhood is especially worrisome, and it is important that if you are feeling this way, you find a trusted adult to discuss it with. Those helping these young girls should work to explore the realities of motherhood with them and help them to be sure they are making their choice with their heads as well as their hearts.

Taking Inventory

In order to fully explore the possibilities for the future, you need to closely examine your life and your views of family, your abilities to parent and your support system. Then consider how they may change in the future. Each woman has her own list and must evaluate the certainty of each component. However, the following list will give you an idea of the things to consider.

- ◆ Your income and how it may or may not change when the baby arrives.

- ◆ Where you will live and if it is suitable for a child. Additionally, whether or not the living arrangement will work for the long term or only for the short term.

- ◆ Your emotional stability. Are the stresses in your life manageable? Will the added stress of caring for an infant be too much?

- ◆ Your view of family. How do you feel about two-parent versus single-parent households? What experiences as a child did you have that are important to you?

- Your knowledge of parenting. Do you understand the needs of an infant, a young child, even a teenager? Will you be able to provide for these needs?

- Child care needs. Will you be staying home with the baby, or will you be able to make other child care arrangements? Can you afford to do either?

- Your future needs. You should have a future as well. Children learn by example. What will you be doing with your life to inspire your child?

- Your child's future needs. Caring for an infant is very different from caring for a moving, talking child. Children grow and need new clothes, materials, and activities to promote their learning.

- Support from your family. Just how much will you ask of them? Is it fair to do so? How much are they willing to help: financially, with housing, providing child care?

- The child's father. Is he involved at all? How supportive is he of your decisions? What financial, emotional, and physical support will he be willing and able to provide? Can you count on him?

- Your sense of self-worth. Do you have the confidence to make decisions for a child? Do you have the confidence to overcome the obstacles and find the solutions? If you are still dependent upon others for your own well-being, it would be difficult for a child to depend on you. Do you believe in your abilities to be a parent?

This is a time to look ahead to your future and envision life both with and without a child. You may find that the support network and the circumstances of your life would be of benefit to a child and thus come to the conclusion to keep your child. You may find conflicting circumstances, strong family support but no financial support, or vice versa. If so, you will have a very difficult choice ahead. You will need to discover if the areas where you lack support will bring undue hardship to a child, or if these areas can be compensated in other ways so as not to negatively affect the child. Finally, some women will find when they take inventory of what they have to offer a child that the obstacles or missing components are too great a sacrifice for the child—and therefore make the decision for adoption.

Even after doing your inventory and seeing the facts fall heavily on one side or another, your instincts may kick in and tell you to do something different. And your instincts may be right. No one can foresee the future with certainty. You only know the way your life is today. You cannot be certain of tomorrow. What you can control is your attitude toward your life.

When instinct tells you strongly to follow a certain path, it can become the ambition behind changing your life. If your instincts are conflicting with the facts ahead of you, take the time to explore why. Is it because you are too scared to face the facts? Or is it because you know in your gut that you can make your life better if you make that choice? If it is fear, then gather more information to determine if your fear is based in reality. If it is your ambitions, gather the information you need in order to make it happen. As you can see, in both cases you will want to look for more information. While you may not be able to clearly find an answer in more facts, you will most likely identify whether or not your instincts are heading you down the right path.

In order to make a decision in the end that you can live with, without regrets, you want to understand what work lies ahead for you if you follow through on that instinct. This is true of any decision we make in life. For instance, while I have been working in the field of child care for almost twenty years, my instincts tell me I should be a writer. My instincts have even gone so far as to tell me I will be on Oprah one day. In order to separate the fantasy from the ambition I researched the literary industry and discovered what it takes to be a writer— even one that gets on Oprah. I know what hard work it is. I know what the odds are, and I know the sacrifices I will have to make—and I still want to write. Armed with information, instinct becomes ambition. (And here I am, writing my second book!)

Let's explore a few scenarios:

Scenario One:

You have no income, but your gut says to keep your child because you want her to know you loved her. When you gather more information about adoption, you see that your child will grow up knowing exactly how much you love her and then feel comfortable with adoption.

Scenario Two:

You have no income, but your gut says to keep your child because you know you are capable of working hard to make the changes necessary in order to raise him. You find a job that will support you both, an apartment to live in, and a child care arrangement. Instinct becomes ambition.

Scenario Three:
You have support from your family, but your gut says to place your child for adoption because you are scared of being a bad parent. When you talk to others and learn more about parenting, you feel more confident and decide you want to keep your baby.

Scenario Four:
You have support from your family, but your gut says to place your child for adoption because you are in school. Your instinct is that you need to finish school and that you are not adult enough yet to be a parent. You gather more information and find that you cannot afford child care and school or that in order to do so you will be completely dependent on your family or working so much your child will never see you. You make the choice for adoption, then dive into your studies determined to improve your life and get out on your own. Instinct becomes ambition.

Your instincts may agree with your inventory; they may differ. They are both pieces of the puzzle you will work on to find an answer. But whether your final choice is to keep your child or to choose adoption, the knowledge you gain in your search will give you the basis from which to make an informed, thoughtful decision—one you can follow through on without regrets.

Taking inventory will require honest, sometimes difficult discussions with your family, friends, and counselors. Gathering all the information you can is vital to making an informed decision. Don't be afraid to ask for help, and be up front with those who offer it—let them know exactly what you need and for how long. It is not fair to simply rely on others to care for you and your child. If you are going to be a parent to your child, then you are responsible for her. It is okay to ask for help. Everyone needs help with something at some point in their life. Still, you need to have a clear plan for how you will come to a point where you are parenting your child on your own without help.

If you are providing support to a pregnant girl or woman who's facing a decision about adoption, remember to be truthful—don't try and sugarcoat your advice or generalize. Be specific. Be honest. Be helpful, but don't do it for her. Give all the information and advice you have to offer, then let her use it to put all the pieces together. You cannot take this journey for her. If you try to force a decision on her or to take on all of the responsibility, you are setting her up for regrets. Help her find all the information and put it on the table; then step back and let her sort it out. She will find her answer.

I read stories now of birthmothers who had such low self-esteem during their pregnancies that they felt as though they had no options. They couldn't see how to rebuild themselves and their lives, much less that of a child, and saw adoption as their only option. In *Waiting to Forget*, Margaret Moorman shares her process for the decision: "I thought of myself as stupid, careless, and contemptible, and I had no sympathy for such a person, who had brought misery not only upon myself but on two families as well. The baby's only hope was to go to someone else as quickly as possible and be spared any further contamination."

While I can relate to her feelings of stupidity and carelessness, it has become clear to me just how important the family surrounding a girl or woman is in her ability to make a decision. It goes much further than what pressures the family puts on her in making a decision about adoption. It encompasses a lifetime of lessons taught and of support, or lack of support, for her self-esteem.

I understand now that I did feel self-empowered at the time of my decision because I had had family support all my life. When I had to put all my cards on the table and make a final decision, I brought my entire past with me: the time my dad trusted me to decide if swimming in a freezing crick in May would be a good idea; the time my mom trusted me to cook supper by myself for the first time; the first time both my parents trusted me to babysit my younger sisters. They had trusted me to make my own decisions many times in my life. They were there to praise me when I made the right choices. They were there to console me when I did not. I was never told I could not try. I was never told I had failed. The words "I can't" were simply not allowed in our household. We were quickly corrected and told to say, "I'm trying; I just haven't figured it out yet." I had been taught to take problems head on and fully explore my options, accept responsibility for my decisions, and learn from mistakes as I fixed them. Dad was forever reminding us that "a mistake is only a mistake until you fix it—then it's a lesson."

If you haven't had this type of support in your life, then let me give it to you. You can do this! You will find the answer that is right for you. Get the facts, follow your instincts, put everything you have learned to this point in your life in one pot, and see what happens. Take your time—the answer will come to you.

Reacting to Change

Things that seem solid before the pregnancy may begin to erode after the announcement. Fathers leave, jobs are lost, society judges, parents abandon, friends disappear. This creates new challenges for the mother and requires increasing support for her to navigate through the decisions ahead.

An unplanned pregnancy can create extreme emotions in people. Often fears emerge and can take over. Those who would never act in extreme ways under normal conditions may react to the pregnancy in ways that surprise everyone. A parent who was always supportive may pull away, or a parent who was distant may now become involved. A boyfriend who seemed committed may disappear; a boyfriend who seemed unsure may propose marriage. Friends may say they support you yet fall away. Others may emerge and offer a hand. Change will become a large part of your pregnancy, and you will have to find ways to deal with these changes as they occur.

If every curveball you're thrown stops you in your tracks and renders you unable to think clearly, it will be very important to know whom you can count on for support. No one expects you to handle all of this on your own. There are counselors, friends, and family members who are willing to help you get through each step.

Once you've taken your inventory and feel strongly about the choice you've made, it can be very difficult to admit when things have just changed too much to stick to your original decision. Accepting the changes and taking another look is not to accept that you have failed—just the opposite. To concede that circumstances have changed and to be able to reexamine your choice for the sake of doing what is best for your child is a sign of your strength.

Girls and women with little or no self-worth can be especially affected by these curveballs in life. They are in danger of making quick decisions that have not been thought carefully through and often end in regret. It is an emotional journey to explore options and find the right answers for each mother and child. When the strength cannot come from the mother herself, it is imperative that it come from outside sources such as family or counselors.

Handling Pregnancy

The period between finding out about the pregnancy and making a decision is also a time to make a distinction between an unwanted pregnancy and an unwanted child. One does not mean the other. In the beginning, it's overwhelming to find out that you are pregnant at a time when it was unexpected and does not fit into your current plan for your life. We've talked about the issue of deciding if you should keep your child or make a plan for adoption. While you work to make that choice, there is still the issue of how to fit a pregnancy into your life.

The changes that you must face simply to fit a pregnancy in your life may affect your thoughts about keeping the child. Many pregnancies can be difficult—morning sickness, early labor, and many other factors can affect your ability to keep a job or to live alone and care for yourself. You may come to a crossroads where you need help with these tasks. As you'll see, I did! When this occurs it is usually a wake-up call to the realities of how much a child will affect your life.

It is important to take care of yourself during this time. Go to your doctor. If you don't have a doctor ask about prenatal care at the adoption agency, they can help. Follow medical advice. Care for yourself and your child. Nine months is a long time, and as your life is changing, your body will change too. Stay healthy for your child and for yourself. If you are physically active now, it will help you to endure the physical demands of labor. Take birthing classes, and don't forget to eat right.

You may need to make other employment arrangements during this time. It can be difficult for some women to continue jobs that require a lot of standing or physical activity. You may find you are just too tired to work. Or you may find you have more energy than you have ever had before. You may have morning sickness for nine days, or the entire nine months, or not at all. Every pregnancy is different. You will probably hear lots of stories of pregnancies and childbirth from other mothers during this time. Listen and learn, but remember that yours will probably be completely different. I have yet to meet two mothers whose stories are exactly the same.

Not knowing what will happen in childbirth can be frightening. Knowledge is power. Find out all you can so you are ready to handle it. Choose someone you can count on to be there with you as you go through it.

As you take the time to plan for the future, remember to take time for today too. Being pregnant can be a beautiful gift. Take the time to treasure these moments regardless of your final decision. Your child can hear you—talk to him. Sing to her. The more you connect with your child, the more you will want to do what is best for him. It is a myth that connecting with your child will make giving her up more difficult. It is this connection that will give you the strength to do what is right, to be able to put the infant's needs before your own, and to reach a decision you will stand by, without regret.

Loving Your Child

Putting a child's needs before your own strong emotions is one of the most difficult tasks in this journey. But as your child grows inside you, you may begin to feel the kind of love only a mother can know. This love you may feel for your child can be channeled in two ways. Your love might make giving up your child too difficult for you to consider it. Or your love might lead you to a deep sense of responsibility to do whatever is necessary so that your baby has what he needs for a full and happy life—whether it is with you or with adoptive parents. Simply put, it will lead to a choice based on either your needs or your child's.

I want to clarify here that choosing adoption because you want to continue school or move ahead in your career or any other goal you were working on that motherhood would make difficult to accomplish is not a selfish decision. It does not mean you love your child any less than yourself. How you will feel is very important! If you are resentful or depressed or stressed because of your decision to keep your child, this will affect the child. Children need strong parents, parents who wholeheartedly are happy to have them in their lives, parents who are proud of themselves and are able to teach self-confidence to their children. You are making a choice based on your child's needs by considering your own feelings too.

These emotional pulls are exactly why the support of family and productive counseling is so important. As we've discussed, often the circumstances in a mother's life change after the pregnancy is announced, and staying focused on considering the child's needs as these changes are inventoried can become very difficult without outside input. The family and/or counselors will need to become the "voice of reason" for the mother, guiding her to face the realities of her life and that of her child in order to make the best decision for both.

This may be a traumatic time for every member of your family. Extended family members may express their own love for the child, making it difficult to follow your heart if you feel adoption is the right choice. Conflicts about the decision may arise. The problems may bring your family closer together: everyone may pull in to protect each other and support each other. Or the problems may tear you apart, and individuals may be unable to face the realities of the obstacles ahead. Counselors need to be very aware of the mother's family interactions, and if a girl or woman does not have an intensification of support from family, it is vital that her counselors provide it for her. Just as the baby deserves to be loved, so does the mother.

Like many mothers whose first instinct is to keep their child, I too was convinced in the beginning that it was the only choice. I loved my baby, and at the time my inventory seemed solid: good job, supportive father of baby, supportive extended family, a home. But as the weeks passed, I faced new obstacles that needed to be seriously considered and inevitably affected the course of my decision.

FACING MY CROSSROADS

The day after telling Brad, I went into work feeling strong. My parents hadn't killed me—yet. Brad said he was going to be supportive. I had a successful business that would keep my future on track. The nausea started to subside, and I got back into my routine of working all day and dancing all weekend with my friends. Mom kept asking if I'd go talk to someone at Catholic Charities about adoption, and I just kept putting it off.

A year earlier I thought I was the luckiest girl in Dubuque. Getting a job doing layout and design had been my dream throughout high school, and it was the degree I was working toward at Clarke College. After my first year of college I landed a job as layout artist at a small print shop. Being from a town where most people retired from the first job they ever got, I was naive enough to believe I was set for life and promptly dropped out of school. After six months the owner of the print shop announced he was shutting it down. The business manager, Rob, and I decided to pool our money and buy the equipment in order to start our own company. I was beyond excited at having this kind of opportunity at nineteen years old. After much discussion, my parents agreed to back me so I could qualify for a business loan, and within the month we had moved to a new location and

become incorporated. I held a business card that declared I was co-owner of ABC Printers, Inc. It was my dream come true.

Six months into owning the print shop, despite being three months pregnant, I relished every bit of work that came my way. I loved sitting at my light table, with orders hung on the wire above it, putting together designs, laying out pages for brochures, and letting my creative juices flow. I spun around on the top of my stool just for the fun of it now and then. Time flew by. I was bouncing between the typesetter, the dark room, my light table, and the front counter. Then late one day I popped over to the printers to chat with our pressman.

"Hey, Jack, how's it going?" I quipped, hopping up onto the table full of paper waiting to be loaded in the press.

"Busy." Jack liked to keep things simple. His unruly hair just poked above the top of the printer as he talked to me from the other side.

I walked around and handed him some paper. "Hey, have you seen Rob? He left for lunch, and I don't think I saw him get back."

"Nope." Jack started moving quickly around the printer now, slathering more ink onto the rollers. I always loved watching this process and respected his precision as he spread it evenly and got the rollers moving again

"We've got some paper orders that need to be done and some bills that came in the mail today. I was hoping to talk to him." I hopped off the table and started handing more paper to Jack.

He took the stack from my hands, and his eyes caught mine as he said, "I don't think it'll do you much good to talk to Rob about the bills." Then he nervously turned away and put his attention back on the press.

"What's that supposed to mean?" I asked. Jack looked at me again. This time I saw sadness in his eyes. He was a hard-working, honest guy, and you could always tell if a secret or problem was weighing him down. We'd become close friends and spent time together after work just chatting and sharing our problems. I touched his arm. "Jack, talk to me."

"He'd kill me if he found out I told you."

I pulled him to sit on the table next to me. "What's going on, Jack?"

He looked straight at me, his eyes black as our darkroom, and it all came spilling out. "Rob has been moving money from your tax savings account into his private accounts. He's planning on taking off on you and moving to Colorado." He let out a deep sigh, as the stress finally drained from his face.

I think I had stopped breathing. Jack took my hands. "I don't know any details or if he's really doing it or just being an ass bragging about how he could do it, but I wanted you to know so you could check it out."

Somehow the lack of oxygen did nothing to stop my heart from beating. It was pounding so loudly in my ears I thought they would burst. I finally found my voice as I gasped in some air.

"What are you talking about? Are you joking?"

"No," he answered simply. "Just check it out." He

hopped off the table and with a few swift movements shut down the press, pulled out the finished flyers, and popped them into a box, slapping on the order label. He started washing down the press.

I finally kicked into gear. "What the hell are you talking about? What money is he taking? Is this why he won't look at the bills? Is the money all gone? When was he planning on leaving? How broke are we? How long have you known? My God, we just had a HUGE month! We were going to be in the black before the end of our first year! How can he do this? We were just talking about opening a second store! Did his girlfriend talk him into this? Where the hell is he right now?" The combination of pacing and screaming finally got the best of me. I got dizzy and quickly grabbed a chair. I started crying and suddenly felt nauseated. "Don't you go anywhere!" I screamed as I ran for the bathroom.

Minutes later I came out and quietly sat next to Jack again. "I'm sorry," I said. "I shouldn't be screaming at you."

"I'm sorry, too," Jack said. "I didn't mean to make you sick."

I started crying again. "Jack, I'm pregnant." I looked through my tears at his shocked face.

"God, are you okay?" he asked as he put an arm around me.

I straightened up. "I'll be fine," I said, "Just as soon as I take care of this mess."

"I really don't know much," Jack said, "But I couldn't sit back and not tell you."

"Thanks," I said. "I appreciate it. I won't say anything

to Rob. Give me some time to check things out, and I'll let you know what I find." I stood up and started helping Jack to clean up. When we finished, he gave me an awkward hug and said, "It's cool you're having a baby." He smiled and left.

I sat at the office desk and took a deep breath. There was only one way to get to the truth. I called Mom.

Hours later I was letting Mom in the front door, locking it behind her. We worked quickly and quietly. Her ten years' experience as a bookkeeper guided her to the right files and ledgers, and it wasn't long before I had an answer. It was true. Rob had taken money from our tax savings account, and instead of sending it to the IRS for our quarterly payments, he was writing the checks to himself. The checks require both of our signatures, but many times he had asked me to sign a few checks—telling me he would be paying bills with them—and I did so before they were made out. Live and learn.

Mom and I agreed to keep a lid on it until we had a chance to talk to our attorney. The business was incorporated, and she wanted to see if that would help protect me. So the next day I came to work with a smile on my face and went to work. I avoided Rob as much as possible and passed by Jack a few times to whisper, "Don't worry. I've got it under control." I had made an appointment for the next day with our attorney. It would be a long twenty-four hours.

The next morning I came to work thinking things couldn't possibly get worse. Never send a challenge out to fate. The phone rang. It was a representative from the

IRS wondering why we were ignoring our last two payments.

That afternoon Mom and I met with the lawyer who had set up our incorporation. I was given two choices. One: stay and fight it out with Rob, work hard to get the business back on its feet, and risk a possible bankruptcy on my record. Two: sign over my half of the business to Rob, leaving him with the nightmare he had created, and walk away.

I was scared. Scared to end up holding the bag and ultimately ruin my credit and any possibility for financial success for quite some time. Scared to let go of all the work I had put into it so far and find myself without a job, still paying on a business loan with no business to support it.

My dreams dissipated like early morning mist after Mom and I left the lawyer's office. In the end, we decided it was best to walk away. Jack had already started to look for another job. I told him he could use my name as a reference, and we agreed that he would stay and act surprised when Rob announced I had left. I wrote all the appropriate letters, collected my things, gave Jack a big hug, took one last look at the little print shop I had so much pride in, and closed the door behind me for the last time.

Mom and I began to sift through my financial mess, and I decided to call Brad to let him know what was going on. No answer. It had been weeks since I had talked to him.

Financially, my life was unraveling. The business was gone, the bills were not. My parents encouraged me to

come home. This was something I had vowed never to do. I was still sure I was keeping the baby, and I knew I would get another job soon. But I had to admit that things were beginning to get complicated, and the idea of returning to the one place I felt safe and protected relieved a large portion of my stress. So I agreed that, for now, I would come home. Just to give myself some time to get everything back in place. Dad joked about how everyone should get at least one chance for a "do over," and that he knew my coming home was just a rest stop on my road to the future. His confidence in me gave me the strength to accept their offer without shame and use it for what it was—not an escape from my problems, but a safe place to think them through and then tackle them head on.

So with no business, no money, and no idea where to start over, I boxed up my things and used my parents' van to move, and within the month I was back on the farm. I had been proud of my independence and being self-sufficient. Now I was admitting defeat. I couldn't do it alone anymore. I wasn't "fine." I tried to call Brad again. Still no answer.

Being home brought back some great memories. Not much had changed. The small rooms of our hundred-year-old farmhouse were full of memories of good times and love. The kitchen where Dad and I hung all of the pictures way too high on the wall to tease Mom—they looked fine to us at six-four and five-eleven, while Mom at five-six thought they were way off. The bathroom downstairs, where Dad had built our first shower. The bathroom upstairs, where he had us four girls line up

side by side to brush our hair in order to measure how big of a mirror to build so we'd stop fighting. The living room with our old upright piano that we had spent hours hovering around, singing old tunes, hymns, and Christmas carols. The bedrooms and the steep narrow stairs that led up to them, reminding me of how Dad would call out "Up the golden stairs!" when it was bedtime. The horse pasture I could see out my bedroom window—and sitting in it in the summer evenings to talk to my pony. The closed-in side porch that served as our playroom and the old cast-iron wood stove Dad put in it so we could continue our play into the winter. The small front porch that Dad had built a railing on, where Mom had planted geraniums in a hanging basket off the beam above it each spring for as long as I could remember, while dozens of kittens gathered around her feet waiting to be the first to play with it.

And my favorite—the huge maple tree in the front yard. I had grown up in that tree. The branches were so wide you could easily walk across them. Mom would pack us lunches and snacks to eat while sitting on the longest horizontal branch that stuck out across our sidewalk. Dad built a deck that circled the entire tree, but he never let us build a tree house in it or even nail boards to make a ladder going up into it higher, because we were to respect the tree's beauty, not harm it. We only had ten acres, but we had managed to squeeze onto it my three horses, a handful of cows and pigs, a couple of acres of corn, a dozen or so chickens, a growing collection of rabbits and cats, and around a hundred ducks that would follow my dad as he did evening chores in a line so long it

would start in the barn behind Dad and end hundreds of yards away at the bottom of the valley in the creek. Then there was the king of the beasts, our three-legged dog, Sparky.

I loved our farm. I loved being with my sisters and watching them go through the years I had already lived there. But my carefree days of childhood were over, and watching my younger sisters enjoying all our family and farm had to offer just left me feeling more defeated. I had worked so hard to move forward with my life, to grow up, to become independent and create my own space in the world the way my parents had for us. Taking this huge step back was devastating. I moped around a lot, watched stupid soap operas alone, and walked aimlessly around the barnyard.

I spent hours sitting on the back of my pony Dusty, telling him all my troubles and crying into his thick, multicolored mane, just the way I had when I was little and had a bad day at school. He looked like a bear, his winter coat coming in thicker every year, and it always made my problems melt away to snuggle into the deep fur. Even though my legs could hook under his stomach, he didn't seem to mind that I had grown. He nuzzled his soft gray nose into the crook of my neck. A couple of times I went riding on my horse Brandy, but Mom didn't think it was a good idea, so I had to stop. Brandy had been my eighth grade graduation present, a beautiful Arabian bay who would prance and hold her head up high just for the fun of it. She was pregnant when we got her, and her foal, Casey, had a long, curly, blond mane. Our vet said that he had never seen anything like it before. I'd watch

Brandy and Casey run through the pasture, side by side, kicking and tossing their heads as they played. I imagined my child and myself riding them together and the dual mother/child group racing through the alfalfa fields.

As time passed, and my circumstances of no job and no home felt more insurmountable, I began to feel out of control. Hopeless. As if I had no options. I walked around in a depressed daze and just kept hitting a wall. I started to listen to Mom talk about adoption and let her lead me toward it because I felt powerless to fight it. After I admitted that adoption might be a possibility, Mom convinced me that I shouldn't get a regular job in the community, just in case I wanted to keep it a secret. I resumed crying myself to sleep each night.

Sitting around the house every day was just too much for me. I had gone from ambitious business owner to a couch potato. I couldn't do it anymore. My options were slim. Mom and Dad were convinced I shouldn't try to get another layout and design job. I understood that it wasn't so much that they were ashamed of me but they worried that if I chose to give up my baby, it could be very painful for me if someone who had seen me pregnant and didn't know about the adoption asked how my baby was doing. It would be easier not to have to explain myself or to face those who would judge me without knowing my entire story.

I agreed, so I got a job babysitting full time for a friend of my aunt, something I had been doing for many summers between school years. The family was terrific. They had three amazing little girls I soon fell in love with, and I found myself laughing and enjoying the days again.

We did art projects, played in the grass, soaked up the sun, read every Care Bear book ever published at least twice a day, practiced writing, baked cookies, and braided hair.

I had always loved being with children; it was easy for me to entertain them, teach them, and care for them. Their parents were kind and considerate. They would ask how I felt, paid me well, and showed their appreciation for all I tried to teach their children. Being with people who were not judging me, not pressuring me about my decision, and simply being my friends was refreshing.

Between moving home and going back to babysitting, I felt more and more like the little kid I used to be—someone dependent on Mom and Dad, someone who had no worries and no responsibilities. But as the days passed, and my belly grew, I had to face reality. I was an adult, and I had a huge responsibility ahead of me, and I was not going to pass it off to my parents like a little girl.

I tried off and on to find Brad. I thought if I could re-move just one of my obstacles, I would be closer to mak-ing things work. But no luck. For all I could tell, either he was long gone in another state, or his family and friends were doing one fantastic job of covering up that he was still around. I finally gave up.

Although I didn't have a dream job anymore, I didn't discount the idea that I could get one again after the baby was born. Some days this would bring me hope; other days, like on Sunday, when I read the "help wanted" section of the newspaper, my hopes would fall. The unemployment rate in Dubuque at the time was al-most three times the national rate. I began to feel like a

failure. I had my one shot at a career in this town, and I had blown it. I had spent enough years watching my dad scrape for a job after the construction company he worked for had closed to know that a second chance might be slow in coming.

Although I was frustrated, I soon realized that I didn't have time to wallow in self-pity. I had work to do. I had to fix this. I had to find out exactly where I stood now, get information to find out what possible solutions there were, and make a decision that would get my life, and my baby's, back on track. Somewhere in all this mess was a lesson, and I was bound and determined to find it. I tackled it like any other job I had to do: gathering information and advice but ready to make the decision myself, follow through on it, and learn from it.

In many ways this approach not only helped me make my final decision but helped keep me moving. The busier I got with the intellectual journey, the less time I had for the emotional one. This was not a decision I could explore with my heart. For my heart, the decision was already made—I would keep him. I would love him. We would have each other forever, and the rest didn't really matter.

But the rest did matter. My family had supported my abilities my whole life, enough so that I could not ignore the fact that I had a brain and I knew how to use it. I was done with making mistakes; it was time for the lesson to begin.

Chapter Three

CHOICES THAT LAST FOREVER

The decision-making journey is a time when everything from your life before the unplanned pregnancy comes together. Your past and what your ideals are of family and responsibility. Your sense of independence, level of strength during conflict, capability to make thoughtful decisions, and ability to think in a completely selfless manner. All these traits will guide you as you explore your options and find the answer that is right for you and your baby.

To help you through this difficult process, this chapter will cover the following stages of the decision-making journey.

♦ Taking responsibility.

♦ Getting help from a counselor.

♦ Looking at the future.

♦ Exploring options.

♦ Making your choice.

This process can feel overwhelming at times. You may feel the urge to just give up and let others call the shots for awhile. It's okay to feel this way. You may need to take a break from the decisions for awhile. Take your time, but don't give up. This decision will affect the rest of your life. It is too important to skip or to leave to other people. You can make the right decision for you and for your baby. There are people to help you and options to ease your fears. I did it, many others did it, and we're fine. There will be so much more to your story than this one time where you face this decision. This is why I share my story as it evolved over eighteen years, so you can see that life will go on, and you will find your answers over time. My story is there to offer you hope for your own future. Maybe reading it will help you to make your decision.

Taking Responsibility

When I read the stories of birthmothers who have regrets or felt pressure, most often they had someone in their life whom they feared or who removed the choice from them. Many had parents who simply took over and made the decisions, and they felt powerless to go against them. Many had social workers or counselors who did nothing more than lower their self-esteem to the point of hopelessness. Others lived in communities with such overwhelming social dynamics that the pressure to fit in overwhelmed them.

If any of the individuals in my life had been different, I cannot say that my choice would have been the same.

The influence of each person in my life contributed to my final decision. The people in my life gave me information, advice, and—most important—the room and support to make a decision without pressure from others so it would truly be my own. Research and history tell us that a key to the success of an adoption is for the birthmother to be settled and sure of her choice, and that the choice needs to be what her heart and mind tell her to do.

As you reach out to others for help and advice, remember that this is your baby and your life that will be affected by this decision. You are the only person ultimately responsible for making this choice. You owe it to your child to stand up to anyone who tries to force you into an arrangement you feel uncomfortable with. Think of yourself as an advocate for your child. Fight for what will be best for this child. Don't leave this responsibility to someone else—you will be setting yourself up for a lifetime of regrets. Don't expect all the information to fall into your lap. If there is something you want or need, ask for it; look for it.

If there is an option you are searching for, and it doesn't exist, find someone who can help you to make it happen. This is how we developed today's practices of open adoption. Birthmothers like me refused to be cut off from their child forever and stood their ground until the adoption agencies listened. Only you know what it is you need. Don't be afraid to find it. Be responsible for becoming informed. Be responsible for learning the lesson that is there to be learned from the mistake of getting pregnant. Be responsible for your child.

Getting Help from a Counselor

There are as many adoption agencies and counselors available as there are possible options for an adoption plan. A lot of wonderful people in this field are just waiting to hold your hand, give you a shoulder to cry on, and answer all your questions. You don't need to do this alone.

Research tells us that "young mothers who receive comprehensive counseling are more likely to choose adoption than young women who did not receive this service" (Buckingham and Derby). Unfortunately, many young women don't get the information they need in order to make a decision, and they are left to make a choice based purely on emotion, with no real discovery of the truths and realities in their life. Or just as bad, they make a choice based on someone else's thoughts and feelings instead of their own, setting themselves up for regret.

When I was attending birthing classes with my mom, all the other girls in the group were young teenagers, and they all were planning to keep their babies. We watched a video that showed one girl who kept her baby, one who kept her baby and later placed the baby for adoption, and one who chose adoption from the start. The girls in the video reflected the girls in our class: the older girls chose adoption; the younger ones kept their babies.

The younger girls in my birthing class seemed to have no idea what they were really getting into. Many of them talked about it as if it were a fun game—this cute little doll they would get would be fun to have around.

One girl said it out loud: "Babies are just so sweet. They smell good and they look at you and smile. They're so easy to take care of because they sleep most of the time." They didn't seem to understand about all the late-night feedings, colic, the spitting up, the blowout diapers, the overwhelming expenses. No one seemed to even consider long-term issues like discipline, toilet training, getting kids to school or running them to soccer practice, and, again, the overwhelming expenses. Only the girls who had been out of school, working and living on their own, seemed to have a truly clear picture of the "real world" waiting for them after the baby was born.

My mom and I became convinced that the young girls were not mature enough to make this decision. It was obvious that they needed to be given more information than their young lives had provided them. We felt sad that the parents of these girls had not done much to guide them in fully exploring the adoption option, or at the least, truly understanding what they faced ahead if they kept their child.

Birthmothers need someone to be there to provide information, love, an ear to listen to their thought processes, and a shoulder for them to cry on as they wrestle with their emotions—and that's it. The actual decision has to be made by the mother; history tells us that anything else will result in years of regret and pain. Still, when the birthmother making the decision is too young to have much actual experience with babies or children, it's critical that her family and counselors help her to understand all the aspects of raising a child.

If you are a young girl facing this decision, trust your counselor to provide you information, and please, listen to the facts. Motherhood is a very difficult and demanding job. It can also be the most wonderful experience of your life. Look at everything—the good and the bad. Concede that there are things about being an adult, and being a parent, that you may not understand—and work to understand them.

It is imperative that those who counsel these girls and women, and the families surrounding them, provide a support system free of bias and judgment, giving them the space they need to explore their choices and find answers.

Professionals who deal with young mothers are beginning to create this type of needed support system. Adoption agencies have changed their tactics and policies drastically in the past twenty years. Most of them offer open adoption and/or a form of semi-open adoption and have registries for adoptees and birthmothers to connect. If the first agency you talk to doesn't offer the support you need or the kind of adoption you are looking for, don't hesitate to look for another one.

The American Academy of Pediatrics issued a statement in 1989 offering guiding principles to physicians to help educate and offer support to young mothers. They encourage the discussion of all options available and state, "All of these options should be explored. Their discussion should be open, informative and nonpreemptory." They instruct physicians to find help for their patients: "All nurturing and supportive people, such as social workers or clergy, can then be mobilized to assist in the solution of this problem."

Catholic Charities, the adoption agency that I used, has undergone drastic changes as well. When I went to them back in 1984, open adoption was unheard of, and even semi-open adoption was a new concept. I was lucky enough to connect with Nancy Kinley, a counselor who was a maverick in the agency and who advocated heavily for connections between birthmothers and adoptive families. She had started the tables turning, and I was able to join the few before me who opted for a semi-open adoption. Now Catholic Charities not only supports semi-open adoptions, in which birthmothers and adoptive families share information on an annual basis, but also supports fully open adoptions, in which birthmothers and adoptive parents meet and continue a relationship after relinquishment.

You live in a time when you have numerous options. You can get much more comprehensive and effective information and support from your adoption counselor than in the past, regardless of what choice you make in the end. You will learn more and have more choices than women have ever had before. Use this fact. Accept the advice and help you are offered, and arm yourself with the information you need.

Looking at the Future

It is also during this time that your inventory list becomes the most challenged. When items in your inventory change, you will have to take the time to reevaluate your future. Your emotions may change as well, and you may reevaluate your decision. Even if your inventory or instincts have not changed, it will be important to consider how they will change in the future.

It is crucial for you to take the time to play out the possibilities both for now and for the long term. Looking at each choice not as an answer to a current problem but as the stepping stone to a future will be key in creating a successful outcome.

When my inventory list began to fall apart, I was lucky enough to have people around me who made me take notice. While it was becoming more obvious that adoption would be the best option, no one pushed. This allowed me to make my own decision—and stick to it. They asked tough questions, pointed out realities, laid every card on the table for me to examine, and let me learn on my own just what it takes to be a great mother—the love to do what's best for my child.

It can be difficult to accept a new option if you were settled with your first. But holding on to a decision that was based on facts that are no longer true is foolish. Making a choice based on a current situation, when you cannot be sure it will not change after the baby is born, is equally foolish. Your baby depends on you to be realistic and have a solid plan for his future. Your baby doesn't need a home for six months—he needs it for his entire childhood. She doesn't need food for a year—she will always need it. Look down the road, and see how each option may play out in your life and your child's.

I want to point out again here that it's all right for you to consider how each option will affect your life as well—in fact, it's essential. Thinking about your future will help you to think about your baby's future too. Your baby will need a parent who is strong and capable, who can teach him or her by example how to be a self-sufficient, contributing adult in our society. If you cannot see yourself as progressing with your life and improving as a person when considering a particular option, then it may not be the one to take. You want a bright future for both you and your baby. Imagine the possibilities in the years ahead and find it.

Exploring Options

When you read my story in this chapter, you will see how limited my options were—yet I still had a successful arrangement. You will have so many more possibilities! I am very excited for you because with so many options, you will have a much stronger possibility of creating a successful arrangement.

If you choose to keep your child, the options will vary greatly depending on where you live, what your income status is, and what amount of support from your family you have. However, most places offer some type of support or help for single mothers, whether it is child care at the schools or assistance with food, housing, or utility costs. Your social service agency will be able to provide you with this information.

If you choose to relinquish your child for adoption, you will find a lot of different options as well, but they don't vary quite so much by where you live. Practices may vary at different agencies, but in general, the following steps will occur. First, you will meet with a counselor to discuss your views and opinions. You may meet with your counselor several times as you go through the process of deciding whether or not to choose adoption for your baby. Your counselor will help you to find families who share your opinions and goals. You will be given a brief biography of them and usually a letter from them as well. This will be their chance to tell you about how they feel about you and the adoption arrangement. From here you will be asked to narrow it down to a few families, and you will receive some type of portfolio or scrapbook that they have prepared. Most often these are filled with photos, but usually families also write in them to tell you more about their family and their lifestyles.

At this point you will be asked to choose a family. At most agencies you will only meet with this one family. Keep in mind that these families are very anxious to be chosen and to bring a child into their homes. It is very emotional for them as well. Many have tried to have a child for years, only to be disappointed. Many have been waiting on the list at the adoption agencies for years as well. To get up their hopes by meeting with them face to face when you are really not committed would be unfair. Wait until you've made your decision to get this far in the process.

You will be given the choice to meet the potential adoptive parents, or not to. In most cases birthmothers choose to meet the parents, but you should do what is best for you. At this meeting you may wish to bring some sort of support person. This may be the birthfather, or it may be one of your parents. The counselor is usually present. You will talk in advance about who will be there, so there are no surprises for anyone and everyone feels comfortable with the arrangement.

You may meet at the agency office or in a more neutral place such as a restaurant. Again, you can give your opinion as to where you would like it to take place. At this meeting you will have a chance to talk with the parents and ask them any questions you have. Everyone has different priorities, and I think it's important you think about what is important for you to know. I don't want to give you a list of questions because at this point you should be following your instincts. You've been given all the facts and figures about this couple; it's time to let your heart decide.

I also think it's important for adoptive parents to understand this. I gave a lecture last summer at an agency, and an adoptive mother spoke to the group just before I did. She talked about how shocked she was to find out that a birthmother had chosen to meet with her and her husband because she saw in their portfolio that they had cats, and the birthmother had three cats of her own that she loved dearly. The adoptive mother went on to say she was equally surprised at the meeting when the birthmother asked them questions about the activities they liked to do. The adoptive mother thought she should have asked more business-like questions such as: "Will you stay home with the baby or use child care?" or "Can you afford to provide for a baby's needs?" What this adoptive mother did not seem to understand was that the birthmother already knew the answers to those questions. Simply by being on the list at the agency the birthmother knows that the family has met certain criteria. After reading the letter and seeing the portfolio, the birthmother finds that most of her other practical questions are answered. The birthmother knows that any family she meets will be financially able to raise a child and that they are anxious to have a child to love. She knows they can provide her child with all her child needs. What she doesn't know is if she can trust them.

When you are meeting strangers and looking for a way to trust them, the surest way is to find a connection with them. That's what that birthmother did when she saw the photos of the cats in the portfolio. That's what you need to do. And here I am talking to both the birthmothers and the adoptive parents reading this. This meeting is your chance to reach out to each other and take those first steps of trust. Find a way to connect, make it a starting point, and you will find a way to build a relationship from there.

For me this took huge amounts of time because we only corresponded through letters. You will have a chance to do in minutes what took my son's parents and me years to do. You will be able to reach out to each other and find a connection, begin to build a trusting relationship, and show each other respect all in one meeting.

This is why these meetings will be different for each group of people. Only you know what is important in your life, only you know the types of things that make you feel connected to other people. It may be having similar hobbies, it may be having similar families, it may be your height or the fact that you play piano or sing out of tune. Whatever that thing is, talk with each other, and see if it's there. You'll know if it is.

If after this meeting you decide the connection wasn't there, your counselor will help you to go back and take another look at your choices. Take your time. It's okay to feel unsure, and no one should pressure you into picking just anyone. If you are to build a respectful relationship that will last for years with this family, then you have the right to get it off to the best start possible.

If you do connect at this meeting, you will then begin to discuss your birth plan and your expectations of openness in the adoption arrangement. Be honest. Tell them what you are comfortable with and what you don't want. Be open to their feelings and opinions as well. This is a great opportunity to show each other from day one that you will respect each other. Find a plan that works for everyone. Don't try to dictate the situation. Be open to compromise, but don't compromise on anything you feel strongly about. Until you have relinquished your child (legally placed him or her for adoption), you have the right to make decisions for the baby and yourself. We will discuss possibilities for a birth plan in the next chapter. For now, understand that your feelings are important and will be respected.

You have so many options. The possibilities for you are limited only by your imagination. Think of your best-case scenarios—for keeping your baby or for choosing adoption—and talk to your counselor about them.

Making Your Choice

As you explore your options and come to conclusions, remember that this will be your choice. It may be very difficult to do this; you may feel pressure from your family or friends to choose something else. Where you live, there may be a social stigma for or against a particular choice. Pressure from society has always existed and probably always will. This is why it is so important to rely on your counselor for an unbiased view. Those who have been in the adoption field for years understand the mistakes of the past. They have seen how having a "one-size-fits-all" approach did more harm than good.

We have come a long way. Adoption today is considered a deliberate choice made by the birthmother because she feels it's the best option for herself and her baby. But making that choice is becoming more and more difficult to do as society builds pressure to choose other options. The pendulum has swung from adoption as the first option in an unplanned pregnancy to adoption being the last option. Women are being faced with pressures to keep their baby at all costs, and I worry that years from now we will find (as we did with closed adoptions) that the cost was too high.

Regardless of the specific societal trends, one thing remains true: society as a whole has an opinion as to what is the "best" decision for a young, unwed mother to make. In *Waiting to Forget*, Margaret Moorman discusses the reasoning behind her decision for adoption and that of other birthmothers of her time. She says that young women of her time chose adoption "because society expects her to do so, because she has been told it is the best solution."

It's time for society to let the girls and women facing this problem make the decision for themselves. It is likely you will face pressure from the current trend to keep your child. I offer this insight to help you understand why this may be happening: the majority of adults today grew up in the era of closed adoption. They grew up hearing the stories of pain and regret. They had friends who were forced into giving up their children. They had families who were torn apart and are now searching for each other. The thought of having someone else they care about—you—go through such a negative experience is frightening to them. I don't blame them a bit. But what you need to remember is that was then and this is now. Adoption today is very different from what it used to be. It can be an experience filled with love, respect, and understanding. You owe it to yourself and your child to explore what adoption means today and to educate those in your life about it as well.

About two years after I had placed my son for adoption, I was at a hospital for a test, and as I sat in the waiting area, I noticed a very young, very pregnant girl sitting a few seats away, crying. I scooted over and smiled at her and asked if she was okay. She began to tell me about how she was there for an ultrasound. She was seven months along. I noticed immediately that no one was with her. She started to say that she wasn't sure if she should keep the baby but that her parents wanted her to. Her mom had told her it would be awful to give away a member of their family. It was clear in the few minutes that we talked that the decision had been made for her and that no one had really listened to what she wanted.

I asked her if she had thought about adoption. She said that she did, but what scared her was thinking she could never hear from her baby again, never know if he was okay, never hold him. She didn't think she could do it that way. I told her my story. I explained to her that adoption had changed a lot in the past few years and that she could not only hold her baby but also have on-going communication with the adoptive parents if she wanted. I asked if she had ever talked to a counselor at an adoption agency. She said no. Her parents had been making all the decisions. I told her about Catholic Charities. I made her write it down. I told her about my counselor and how she let me work things out for myself and that there was never any pressure to choose any-thing.

I tried my best in those few minutes to let her know that she did have other options and that even though she might still decide to keep her baby, she owed it to her child and to herself to explore all the options. Most im-portant, she needed to make the decision herself. She seemed to be relieved to be able to talk to someone who listened to her. She had seemed so powerless in those first moments we met. When it was time for her to go, she seemed hopeful.

I prayed for her for a long time after we met. I still think of her often and wonder what happened. I wonder if she had the courage to go to an adoption agency, or if her parents' pressure was just too much for her. I wonder what her final choice was, and if it wasn't her own choice, how much pain and regret she has felt. I pray that whatever happened, as she grew older she found someone who would truly listen to her and give her a way to heal.

Armed with the truth and information you will be able to stand up to any pressures you face and forge ahead on a path designated as your own. You deserve a future without regrets. When you make the choice your own, when you know without a doubt that you have explored all your options, you've gathered all the information, and your gut is telling you it's right, it will be one you can stand by. Your resolve and confidence in your decision will be what helps you to get through the difficult times, and you will get through them. Be proud of yourself for doing the hard work and making the hard decisions.

MY LESSONS

Where to start? With the facts. Fact: I was going to give birth to a baby. Fact: I had no real career at the time. Fact: I would not be marrying the father. Fact: I had no home of my own. Fact: I was a talented person

with a good prospect of obtaining a decent job again. Fact: If I did get a job, someone would have to care for the baby. Fact: If I didn't get a job, I wouldn't have the income needed to raise a child. Fact: I loved this baby. Fact: I knew what it would take to care for a child, giving him love and supporting his growth and development, and I felt confident that I could do it.

A mix of good news, bad news. As I started to jot down these facts, I came to one where I got stuck. Fact: My family will support my decision and me. Emotionally, there was no question. My dad's big shoulder was always available to cry on, and my mom would always be there to listen. But would that be enough? Did I need more from them? Would they be willing to make sacrifices in order to show their support? Time for another talk with my parents.

These questions were some of the toughest—not just to get an answer to—but to ask in the first place. Mom wasn't at home raising kids any more. She had moved ahead with ambitions of her own and had a career she really enjoyed and was proud of. Dad worked on highways and could be away for weeks on a job. Keeping the baby would mean someone had to provide financial security, and someone had to care for the baby. I couldn't do both. While Brad had said he would be supportive, I had no delusions about his providing child care, and since I hadn't heard from him in weeks, I was beginning to wonder just what his idea of "supportive" was.

If I went back to work, could I ask Mom to quit in order to raise her grandchild? If I stayed home with the

baby, could I ask Dad to support us financially? Even though I had moved home, I knew it was considered a temporary fix. Would they consider letting me live there with a baby long term? They had both obviously transitioned to a life without young children under their roof, with more options for their time and money because of it. Could I, should I ask them to give that up? If I did, would they?

Independence was a gift my parents had given me beginning at a very young age. It was something I was proud of personally, and when an act of my independence made my parents proud of me, it was so overwhelming that there would be no way to stop the tears. I had spent many hours trying to earn their pride in this regard. Likewise, I realize now just how many years they had spent trying to instill self-pride in me in this regard. Independence was our family badge of honor and not given up easily. So it was not surprising to me the answers I received in our conversation.

We sat at the kitchen table. It was a beautiful solid wood circle pedestal table, now stained a soft brown, a large improvement over the lime green it had been painted when I was little. And Mom had recently been able to purchase six chairs that matched, finally throwing out the assortment of garage sale bargain mismatches she had had for years. The sun was streaming in through the tall windows. (After I grew up in a house with ten-foot ceilings and long windows, every other home has felt like a small cave.)

Dad's work boots, brown with dried mud, were left by

the screen door, a cluster of kittens piled against the other side. Dad had a firm "This is YOUR mess, YOU clean it up" look on his face, but his eyes gave him away. One look told me he wanted nothing more than to swing me up in his arms and protect his little girl with everything he had. Mom still looked stunned. I'm not sure if she was thinking anything more than "Oh my God" yet. I got the impression that when she looked at me she saw a four-year-old me in pigtails saying *Mommy, can I keep my baby?*

"What will it take in order for me to keep my baby?" I asked her.

"You know the answer to that," Dad answered for her.

He was right, of course. "Could I live here and take care of him?"

"You know we'll help you any way we can, dear," Mom said. "But you'll have a lot of expenses for the baby. Do you really want to go on welfare? How will you keep your career options open? How long do you think you'll be here?"

"I don't know."

"You can't raise a baby on I-Don't-Knows," said Dad.

Mom stepped in. "We know that if you want to do this, you'll find a way, and you'll make it work. We've always been proud of you and what you've done with your life so far. But think ahead a few years. Are you going to be proud of yourself? If you give up on yourself and your own future now, what's left for your child to learn from?"

I knew all of this, and I knew the answer to her question. "Nothing." I looked at my dad. I couldn't remember one moment in which I had not been proud of him and learned from it. Mom too. For a split second I secretly wished they were going to be the parents to my baby. That's what he deserved—the best.

"We want you to think about what you will have to offer this baby, not just how you'll get by. You can't just cover your bases for the first month, or year. Having a baby means forever. You've got to think five, ten, twenty years down the road. This isn't a job you can quit once you start. You've got to be sure."

"I know, Dad. I'm trying to think about it. I just need to know—if I got a job and had to get day care, things would be tight for a while. Can we stay here or not?"

"You know you can," answered Mom.

"And if I went on welfare and got help paying for a place to live, would that be okay with you?"

"This is your decision," said Dad. "You do what you think is right, and we'll help any way we can. We're not going to tell you what to do."

"Thank you, but I do appreciate your advice," I said.

"Are you even considering adoption?" asked Mom.

"Yes," I answered, "but it's hard to think about it. I want to be sure I look at all my options."

"Do you think it's easy for us to even consider having our first grandchild put up for adoption?" Dad was boiling over. "This is very painful. But we care enough to want what's best. This baby deserves a family—a mother, a father, a home, security. Things you can't give right

now and don't know if you ever will be able to provide. Do you realize how much harder it will be for you to meet someone and get married if you already have a child? We're afraid you not only won't be able to provide a family for this baby, but you'll never have one for yourself. We've always wanted to provide something for you girls that was better than what we had growing up. Wouldn't you like to do the same for any children of yours?" Dad sighed and leaned back in his chair. You could see the memories of a tough childhood flash across his eyes and dissipate into the pools of tears forming there. I knew he didn't need answers to his questions. He'd made his point and expected me to get it the first time.

"I can't imagine ever being able to provide a better childhood than the one you gave me." I stood up and hugged Dad, then Mom. "I love you both."

"We love you too," they answered in unison.

"I'm going upstairs," I said. "I've got a lot to think about. Thank you," and I headed for the stairs. As I started up, I could hear Mom start to sob and the scrape of Dad's chair on the linoleum as he got up to go to her. Again, I wished this baby were lucky enough to be a sibling of mine, instead of being stuck with me as his mom.

I began to imagine what life would be like if I kept my baby. I thought about Jenny, a single mother who had lived across the hall from my apartment in town. Her daughter, Stephanie, was the cutest three-year-old I had ever known. Jenny worked a lot and even with welfare was barely keeping financially afloat. She worried about it a lot. Jenny had a boyfriend, Chad. He was not Stepha-

nie's father, and many of the girls in the building revered the fact that he so obviously adored her "anyhow." I prayed they would become a family someday. Stephanie so desperately wanted a daddy. You could see it in the way she turned up the charm whenever Chad was near. When she flashed her cherub smile at him, it broke my heart.

Now, as I remembered them, I put myself in Jenny's place. I was lonely, worried about money, working all the time. I imagined my child wandering into neighbors' apartments looking for friends, someone he could count on, a father. I started crying. I tried to imagine I had gotten a great paying job—but then a scene where I had to leave my baby with a babysitter at a house full of babies and a TV entertaining them all flashed in my brain. I screamed into my pillow.

Eventually, my crying subsided to an occasional sob. I lay in my childhood bed, staring at the plaid curtains that my mom made when I begged her to redecorate my room in high school. I decided that it was time to stop thinking like that kid and start thinking like Mom. My child deserved her, so the least I could do was to start to think like her. Then maybe I could take the first steps to being a good mom and start making some decisions.

The next morning I asked Mom to make an appointment at Catholic Charities. I asked if she would come with me, and I was not surprised when she answered, "Of course."

Nancy Kinley was my counselor. She was funny and kind and seemed genuinely interested in hearing every

word of whatever I wanted to talk about. I looked forward to my sessions with her and would often call her before it was time for our monthly appointment. I could vent about my parents, Brad, feeling sick, my business, everything. And I could cry. At home, I felt the need to hide my crying, to be strong. When I was with Nancy, I didn't hide anything. Some days I don't think we talked much at all; she just let me cry. I never realized how badly I needed to until the door closed and we sat down. When I got it all out, she would always have something positive to say to help me let it go and move forward. This didn't mean she let me off the hook—she asked some tough questions. She made me think. She helped me break through that "everything's fine" façade and face some real issues with real solutions. She helped me get my focus back.

When I first lost my business, I went into such hopelessness that I felt there was no other course but adoption. You'd think this would have my parents and Nancy jumping at me with papers to sign. But they didn't.

I think the reality of my parents' first grandchild entering the world was sinking in, and even they weren't as clear about what I should do anymore. It's always easier to make decisions with your head—once your heart starts to join in the debate, it gets really messy.

I think maybe Nancy got to know me well enough after that first meeting to know that if I made a quick decision, I would probably regret it, or worse, wouldn't stick to it later. She seemed to know that I still had a journey to make and that until I truly came to terms with what future I was choosing and why, I'd never move on. So

step by step, she held my hand and took me down the road.

We kept talking about both options. Up to this point I had considered if I could afford to keep the baby, if I could emotionally handle giving up the baby, and if I would have acceptance and support from my family and church if I kept the baby or chose adoption. Then in December came the session when she asked the toughest question of all: "What do you think your baby would want?"

No one had asked me this yet. I was told what my parents wanted. What my friends wanted. What my church wanted. And none of those opinions were enough to set my mind one way or the other. I didn't really care a lot about what other people wanted. At twenty years old I was too focused on what I wanted. What I felt. What I needed. I thought it was my decision to make and really no one else's business. Nancy pointed out to me that it was very much someone else's business—my baby's.

We started talking about what kind of life I thought the baby would want. I thought of my childhood and how great it was. I couldn't imagine anyone not wanting exactly what I had had. I thought about Stephanie. I remembered the longing I saw in her eyes whenever Chad came over.

Nancy invited me to attend a birthmothers' meeting, where there would be a group of girls who had gone through the experience and could share their feelings with me. Although to Nancy and my mother I stated that I was leaning toward adoption, despite the odds against

me I was still pretty sure I was going to find a way to keep my baby. But I wanted to talk to someone who had gone through this. Somehow I hadn't felt yet that anyone I had talked to truly understood how I was feeling. I was hoping to find someone who could, so I agreed to attend the next meeting.

I sat quietly and listened as six women shared their stories. They ranged from someone who had just had her baby two weeks earlier to someone whose baby was now three years old. Some were getting a letter or a picture each year from the adoptive parents; some were not. Most made their decision during their pregnancy, but one didn't decide until three weeks after her child's birth. I remember being amazed at how different each person's story was. I was expecting to hear one of them tell my story. I wanted to be able to say—that's exactly how I feel! But instead, I heard a wide range of emotions and saw myself not in just one person's story but in a collage of their different stories.

It was a very emotional experience. I cried the entire drive home, and secretly for days after. The reality of my situation was sinking in. There was life after the birth (for both the baby and me), and it wasn't all hearts and roses the way everyone was trying to make me believe, regard-less of which choice I made. My heart ached for the pain that some of the girls shared. Overall, I got the impres-sion that they each felt they had done the right thing, but one thing was very clear: not one of them was forgetting. My family had been emphasizing to me that if I chose

adoption, I would then be able to forget, put it behind me, get on with a normal life. While it seemed the girls at that meeting had indeed gone on with their lives, no one was forgetting a thing.

In fact, instead of long discussions about how their lives were now back on track or how happy they were, they talked about the children they had lost. They shared their worries about their baby's parents, their joys of receiving letters and pictures, their hopes for their baby's lives. No one seemed concerned about whether or not their own lives had turned out okay. Everyone's main concern was that their babies' lives turn out okay. In fact, no one even discussed their own life and what was happening now for them personally.

This was new for me. So far everyone throwing opinions at me did so under the umbrella of what would be best for ME. I was beginning to see now that this decision was really about choosing what would be best for my baby. I learned from those mothers that yes, they did suffer loss, but what mattered most was that their babies would be happy.

I shared all of this with Nancy. I was not surprised that she was pleased at my revelation. She had been leading me toward it for some time now. Caring more about someone other than myself was not going to be an easy task. As a very independent twenty-year-old I could not have been more self-absorbed. But Nancy was patient. She gave me books to read and more meetings to attend, and she spent hours discussing babies with me.

On my own I spent time talking to my baby. I would rock and sing to him. I would rub my growing belly and tell him about his grandparents, his aunts. And I would tell him how much I loved him.

The more I thought of him in terms of the future, the more worried about him I got. The more I worried about him, the more I loved him. The more I loved him, the more I wanted to be sure to do what was best for *him*.

Over time, I realized that one of my biggest fears about adoption was that he, or that anyone, would think I gave him up because I didn't care. That he would think I didn't want him. This thought petrified me. Just the possibility made my blood run cold.

I shared this fear with Nancy, and she gave me a book called *Dear Birthmother*. It was filled with letters from adoptive parents, and some adoptees, to the birthmother. I devoured the book. I read it over and over and over. I cried. Then I read it again and cried some more. This was my first exposure to adoptive parents and their thoughts and feelings. I was surprised by the amount of love and respect they showed toward the birthmothers. And thankfulness. It was overwhelming. My circle of concern was now broadening past myself to include not only my baby but also his prospective parents.

Reading *Dear Birthmother* addressed my biggest fear: would my baby, would his parents really understand how much I loved him? It was clear that they would. I had bought into the myths of adoption: that choosing it meant I didn't love my baby, that my baby would grow up angry with me. The pages and pages of letters written by

birthmothers, adoptive parents, and adopted children all had one underlining theme: love. While society was still attacking me with their conviction that all the myths were true, I knew after reading this book that they most definitely were not.

As my search for a decision continued, Lori and I spent a lot of time together to discuss what I was learning, or to just escape from it for awhile. Some days we'd just go to a movie and out for brownie sundaes at Perkins, the way we had for years, and talk about everyone except me. It was during one of these gossip sessions in January that she told me she had heard Brad had left town and was engaged. I was stunned. I had talked to him just a couple of times on the phone since my announcement, and he had seemed open to whatever my decision was. Regardless of my decision, I had assumed he would be supportive and involved when the time came to follow through on it.

The next day I tried calling him and could only reach his sister. She said he had left the state, and she wouldn't tell me anything else other than he didn't want anything to do with the baby or me.

My house of cards was falling down. Finances and a home were already proving to be obstacles to keeping my baby; now not having a father was added to the list. I couldn't imagine a life without my dad. How could I deny my child that relationship? This was getting harder by the day. I knew my family would help me when I needed it, but I wasn't prepared to ask them to do everything. Without a dad around I knew my father would step up to

the plate, but was it fair to ask him to? Dad would be sacrificing being Grandpa; my child would be sacrificing an actual dad; my entire family would be sacrificing finances, a life with no kids at home, possibly their reputations. If family is meant to support each other and sacrifice for each other, didn't that apply to me as well? Why should they give up so much for me? Shouldn't I be willing to give something up for them? How can I ask a newborn baby to make a sacrifice when as a grown woman I'm afraid to?

Should I be trying to keep our family together at all costs? Even if it "costs" someone in the family? Not in our family. For us, family was about helping each other to be our best. Whatever it was. Everyone. So sacrificing my future in the hope that I could provide a future for my baby was not in line with this value. We were always taught to be our best, to put forth our best effort. Mom and Dad gave us whatever we needed, or asked for, to get us there. When I joined the track team, Dad built me hurdles. When I wanted to enter cookies in the 4-H fair, Mom bought the ingredients and spent days with me showing me what to do, then letting me bake batch after batch on my own until I got it right. When I wanted to open the print shop, they gave me the collateral. And I knew that if I chose to be a mom, they would give me anything I asked for in order to help me to do my best.

But would "my best" be good enough? Could I give up all my ambitions and put a baby's life first? If I did, would I ever regret it, or worse, resent my own child for it? I doubted I would. But if I didn't become my personal

best, would I have anything to offer my child? Would I be able to support him in becoming his own personal best? The pride I felt in my own parents and all they had done for me was overwhelming—would my child feel the same about me?

These questions ravaged my brain for days. Slowly, after hours of praying, I found answers. I couldn't ask my family to make sacrifices, even if they were willing to. I couldn't expect my child to, either. But it had to be more than just doing what was right for my family, or even what was right for my baby. I needed to find the best solution for everyone involved. I understood that a decision for adoption would affect all our lives, not just mine.

I don't remember actually making the decision for adoption. It's not like I woke up one morning and announced to everyone that I was ready to give up my child. The decision had so many layers for me that it went beyond one choice to become a myriad of decisions and concerns.

I didn't just want to give up my baby. I wanted to make a plan for his life. I wanted to control as many issues as I could, to do all I could to make this turn out right. I told Nancy I had to know he was okay. She had asked me to learn to care enough about my baby to put his needs first—I wasn't about to leave it to chance; I had to KNOW.

Nancy said there were some parents willing to share information annually until the child was eighteen. I wouldn't get to meet them or learn their name, but they

would send letters to her, and she would pass them on to me. She cautioned me that sometimes the parents change their mind and don't send letters. That wasn't an option for me. I had to know he was loved, he was happy, he was okay! I decided that finding the right parents for my baby would be the deal breaker. I wasn't just going to give my baby away—I wanted to give him to the right parents for him.

This task was even more difficult than I had imagined. Nancy pulled out a file of prospective adoptive parents. Each page had a short description of their occupations, their ages, and a sentence or two about their lives—no names, no addresses. I had very little to go on. It was frightening. Nancy helped me through it one small step at a time. She gave me a file with dozens of descriptions in it and told me to take it home, look through it, take my time, and see if anything stood out. I did what she asked and came back just as confused a week later. She handed me another file.

I sat on the end of our couch in my parents' living room, looking through the file. I was struck by how many couples were desperately waiting for a child. Nancy had told me that most had been waiting for years, and because there were so many, the older the couple got, the less chance that they would receive a child. This saddened me. It was hard to imagine getting married and never being able to have a family—then to have your hopes up for years and years, waiting for someone like me to see your little slip of paper in a file and answer your prayers.

Then I found a page that said the following:

> Adoptive Father: Age 39. Education: B.A. in Soci-
> ology, 18 hours towards an M.A. in guidance and
> counseling, and a two-year course in dental tech-
> nology. Works part time. Religion: Catholic. Inter-
> ests: Basketball, sailing, traveling and being out-
> doors in general.

> Adoptive Mother: Age 37. Education: B.A. degree,
> M.A. in counseling and a DDS degree. Occupa-
> tion: Dentist. Religion: Catholic. Interests: Read-
> ing, sewing, tennis and watching Iowa football.

> This couple has been married 13 years and has
> no children. They live in a medium-sized town in
> an older home. It is acceptable to them to annually
> share ongoing information and pictures with birth-
> parents until the child is 18 years of age.

What struck me first was their ages. At twenty, I thought thirty-nine and thirty-seven seemed incredibly old. I was amazed that they hung in there and were still waiting. They hadn't given up as they got older; apparently they felt it would be worth the wait. I was also impressed that they were both professionals and had degrees. At that time no one in my family had ever graduated from college.

I also liked the idea that they were dentists. I used to babysit for a dentist in Dubuque. The dentist and his wife were really creative people who had wonderful adventures, great kids, and a beautiful home. I imagined my child becoming a part of that picture. The dad said he liked the outdoors, and the mom was a Hawkeye fan. *I'll bet they have a lot of fun together too,* I thought.

Because I Loved You

As much as I appreciated couples who probably had more to offer financially than I did, as someone who grew up without much money and still had a fantastic childhood, I knew that true happiness for my child would come from having loving parents, not a big house. I liked the idea that they lived in an older home; the farmhouse I grew up in was over a hundred years old. Reading that they had been married for thirteen years told me that they had loved each other a long time. A home full of love was exactly what I wanted for my baby.

The mom especially stuck out for me. The first things listed for her interests were reading and sewing. Those were my own mom's two favorite hobbies too. Tennis meant she was active, and a football fan meant she stepped out of traditional female roles now and then—those were qualities that described ME. I had been praying for a while that my baby could have my own mom instead of me, and now I felt that I had found a mom who was a little of each of us.

I still can't explain exactly how, but the few words on that page spoke to me. I saw a couple who reminded me of my own parents and me, even though on paper we only had a few things in common. It was just this feeling I got. I turned the page and read on, but every four or five pages I'd flip back to that one page and read it again.

On my second visit in February with Nancy, I showed her the page and asked if she could tell me anything more about them. She said that she knew that their priest had highly recommended them, that he said they were very kind and patient and would be devoted and

loving parents. That did it for me. It wasn't a friend, a social worker, a relative—it was a priest who gave this recommendation. I had been praying so hard for so long to make the right choice that at that moment I felt God was stepping forward to say these were the parents he chose for my son. That may sound foolish or dramatic, but it was how I felt, and I am as convinced today as I was then that God hand chose my son's parents. I told Nancy they were the ones.

At my next appointment in March, Nancy told me that she had talked with the adoptive parents and they were elated. She said they had almost given up hope and were very excited. They were more than willing to share letters and photos, and Nancy was confident that I could trust that they would. She also said they asked how I was doing and sent their prayers that the rest of my pregnancy would go well. From the very beginning, they made me feel respected. I began filling out the necessary paperwork.

The decision made, I relaxed and moved forward, savoring the few precious months I would have with my son. I continued babysitting, sitting in the rocking chair every afternoon during the little girls' nap to rock my own baby and sing to him. I told him how much I loved him over and over and over. I talked about the family God had found for him. And I told him about me. I told him about my childhood, my sisters, my parents, my grandparents. I shared family stories, funny anecdotes, and secrets. I sang to him "Skim-a-ra-link-a-dink" and "Jesus Loves Me." Over and over and over.

I referred to the baby as "him" because my cousin and I had decided it was a boy, even though we had no proof. For years we had called each other "Patty Jo" and "Debbie Jo," not because our middle names actually were "Jo" but because we had an aunt who called us by these names and we thought it was funny. They became our secret nicknames for each other. One day during my pregnancy we decided it was wrong to refer to simply "the baby" and that I should pick a name. The choice was easy—it HAD to be a "Jo." So he was.

A couple of months earlier, just after ringing in the New Year of 1985, my grandma was in a near-fatal car crash. She had broken most of her ribs, torn open her stomach, damaged organs; she was barely alive. My grandma and I had always had a special, close relationship. For the first five years of my life I lived a short walk through the woods from her house and had unlimited access to her hugs and cookies. Every summer I spent a week with her, learning to bake, play cards, and talk about everything and everybody.

At the same time that Grandma was in the hospital, my grandfather was brought in for what they thought was appendicitis. Instead, when the surgeons opened him up, they found cancer.

The family was a wreck. Our beloved grandparents were both in pain, and they were not even able to be at each other's side for support. When they were both finally released, it was clear they were going to need help. I had great concern for both my grandparents and wanted to do everything I could to help, so I moved in with them. I

still worked my babysitting job during the weekdays, but I was able to be there every evening and the weekends. I lived with them until the middle of March, a couple of weeks before my due date. Grandma was too tough to stay in bed for long, she was soon running the house (and Grandpa) with her old gusto.

Although on the surface those months appeared as trying times, they really were quite happy. I loved being there with my grandparents, learning from Grandma about baking, how to know what "till it looks good" meant in any given recipe, sharing the food with Grandpa, and watching him tease Grandma. I prayed every day that my child would some day find the kind of love they had. I was pretty sure that I wouldn't.

Chapter Four

No One Forgets

Giving birth changes a woman forever. It is the most personal, emotional, incredible experience she will ever have. It is not an experience that can ever be forgotten or discounted. Women who have chosen adoption can no more easily forget their child than they can forget that they have legs.

Thankfully, we have learned from our past. Between the research and the myriad of talk shows in which birthmothers searching for their children pour their hearts out, sharing memories of their last moments with their children, we know that the experience of giving birth and letting go are too emotionally searing into our hearts to ever be forgotten.

If you have chosen adoption, these moments you will have—giving birth, saying good-bye—will be a very emotional time for both you and your family. Just as you took the time to make your decision for adoption, take the time to plan ahead for the birth, to consider how you hope it will all go. This chapter will help you to piece together your feelings about the different aspects of this time:

- Celebrating the birth.
- Respecting the entire birth family.
- Saying good-bye.

Every experience will be different, but each is to be celebrated. Taking the time to treasure the journey is an important step in the healing process after your child is gone. Accept the support from family and counselors to get the most out of these precious few moments. You have come a long way and grown immensely over the nine months of your pregnancy, and now it is time to take control in taking the time you need to say good-bye.

Celebrating the Birth

As part of your adoption plan, you will also create a birth plan. You will have a chance to talk with your counselor about what you envision for the birth of your child. There is no "right" way to plan this. It varies greatly from birthmother to birthmother. Only you know what you can and can't handle. Only you know what will create a special event. Your counselor will most likely have some type of questionnaire or other form for you to fill out with the details. There is much to consider.

- Who do you want with you in the delivery room? Who do you not want there?
- Will the adoptive parents be allowed to visit you, or just the baby? Or would you rather they not come until you have left?

♦ What extended family will be allowed to visit you or the baby? What extended family of the adoptive parents will be allowed?

♦ Will the birthfather be there? How about his family?

♦ Would you prefer separate spaces for each of the different families, where the baby can be brought to them instead of everyone coming to your room?

♦ Do you want to hold the baby right away? Do you just want to see the baby but not hold her? Do you want the baby to stay in your room or the nursery?

♦ When it is time to leave, do you want to be alone to say good-bye to your baby? Do you want to hand your baby to the adoptive parents?

♦ Who do you want to take you home? Who will stay with you when you get there to help care for you?

As it was with choosing the adoptive parents, you will have many more options than I had. You will be able to decide how much contact, if any, to have with adoptive parents. Most hospitals now have what they call "birthing suites," where you give birth in the room you will stay in and the baby stays there too. If you are uncomfortable with any of these choices, you need to tell your counselor and doctor. If there are any problems with the delivery, such as a caesarean, you will need extra time at the hospital and extra help to get around, even to hold your baby, as you heal.

Of course you should also plan for when your labor begins—how to get to the hospital, what to bring, etc. Your doctor will help you to be prepared. The nurses at the hospital will be there to help you through this as well. Be clear with both your doctor and any nurses on duty about how you are feeling and what your needs are. You deserve their respect during this time as well. If you encounter someone at the hospital who does not show you this respect, then ask him or her to leave immediately, and tell your adoption counselor about it right away. Your counselor can help to be sure you are surrounded by people who will care for you with concern and respect. Don't be afraid to ask for help. This is not a time for you to have to deal with people who want to impose their judgments on you. You have already faced any mistakes you made and learned from them. You are here, willing to do all you can to make it right. You deserve to be celebrated, not chastised.

You should realize that whatever plan you choose, you may very well change your mind after your baby is born. You may plan not to see the adoptive parents, but after the birth you may decide you want to share those moments with them. Or vice versa. You may not think you want much time with your baby, but once you hold her you may not want to let her out of your sight.

Emotions will be running very high during this time. It may become difficult to remember the hard process you went through to make your decision. This is one reason to go through the tough process of gathering information and taking the time to make the decision that is right for you: you will then be able to follow through on it. It will still be hard; nothing can take away all the pain. But if you know in your gut you will be doing the right thing, you will find the strength to carry through.

Remember that you are not alone. Reach out to your support people, and take the help they offer. Take each moment as it comes and find your way. You can do it. You've made it this far. Don't let go of the strength you had to make your choice in the first place. Your baby is depending on you to do what is right. Gather strength from the love you feel for your baby to help you move forward.

Consider all the possibilities for your child's birth, and create a plan that will celebrate the life that has now entered this world and celebrate your strength in being a part of it. Giving a child up for adoption never discounts the fact that he first had a mother who carried him in her womb and cared so deeply for him that she put his best interest before her own emotional needs. In fact, it celebrates that fact. You deserve to be celebrated for the brave and selfless thing you are about to do. Create a plan that celebrates you.

Respect for the Entire Birth Family

Just as no birthmother forgets her child, her family remembers forever also. Placing my son for adoption was a decision that forever altered the future of my family. It had far-reaching effects on each member, some of which I would not fully understand for years to come. While everyone understood that my son would have a family, a mother, a grandmother, aunts, and uncles, no one escaped the deep pain that it would not be us.

In the same way that you will have to determine how you will handle the birth, your family deserves the same respect. This child is someone's grandchild and niece or nephew, and the loss of the child as a member of the family will bring grief to everyone. Adoptive parents who respect this and honor the family that was willing to give them such a precious gift will build a foundation for trust and understanding in an open adoption arrangement.

Talk to your family about how involved they would like to be. Try your best to honor these requests without sacrificing your own needs. They may want to be at the hospital, or they may not. They may want to meet with adoptive families, or they may not. There is such a mix of emotions for families that it can be difficult for adoptive families and birth families to be together. Most often, your counselor will arrange for them to have separate spaces. It's important for adoptive families to remember that birth families will be dealing with a loss—and they deserve to get through this grief in a healing way. Birth families need to remember that the adoptive family has been waiting a long time for this moment. They have overcome many obstacles and will be filled with joy and anticipation for the future—and they deserve the chance to celebrate this. These are very conflicting agendas. Everyone needs to think ahead to this time at the hospital and consider how they can respect one another's needs.

This precious child, who has come from one family and will soon join another, is not a piece of property. This is a person. A person who has black hair because of her mother, who plays the violin like her grandfather, and who skips rocks like her brother. This is a person who hates peas like his aunt or has a birthmark like his uncle. His life began months ago in the body of a woman who cared enough to make a choice that put his needs first. These are all things that adoptees know. This is why those who were placed through closed adoptions still go searching for their birth families. It is very important for adoptive families to know this as well. It is not an issue of love.

It is not competition between parental figures. It is simply the progression of a person's life and the acknowledgment that the birth family was a part of it. It makes no more sense to treat a child as if her life only began at the point the adoptive family brought them home as it is to treat a child as if her life began only once she started kindergarten. Every moment in a person's life counts and should be celebrated. The fact that a child graduates from college will never negate the fact that he once went to preschool. Both happened, and both hold their own unique significance in his life. In the same way, a child who knows that her birthmother loves her will not discount the fact that the people who raised her are her parents. Both will hold their own unique significance in her life.

If you understand this, then everyone involved will have a basis for trusting each other. This trust will grow as you respect and understand one another's point of view. Give this child the best life possible by filling it with respect, love, and understanding from the moment he's born.

Saying Goodbye

I will not kid you. This will most likely be the toughest moment of your life. It will hurt. You may not think you can do it. You may not think you can go on after you have. But you will.

You may be unsure as to how to say good-bye to your child. Again, this is a very personal moment, and only you can know the answer. I believe that you have grown over the nine months of your pregnancy and you are capable of finding your way through this as well.

Some guidelines may help. It has been learned that removing a child before the birthmother has a chance to see him does not save her the pain of letting go. Instead it can intensify those feelings of loss. Adam Pertman writes:

> Today research across the spectrum of human behavior shows that people need to face the searing issues in their lives in order to work through them with a minimum of psychic damage. Denial rarely works, and neither does hiding. In the case of adoption, to put it simply, women who say good-bye without first saying hello generally can't fully process their decisions and therefore never come to terms with them. And knowing their children won't vanish into the ether invariably helps them continue to heal over the years.

You may be unsure about seeing your child, but I am suggesting that you do. Give yourself the chance to see the beautiful life you have created. Be proud of your child. Look at him and see that he is a part of you. You will always be with him because he is made of you. She may have your eyes, your nose. He may have your dimples, your toes. Get a picture of your child in your mind so when she is gone you will remember; you will be able to work through your grief because you will know your child exists and she will be loved. She will not disappear—she will go on to have a full and happy life because of your selfless act and courage.

I understand there may be circumstances where you may feel strongly about not seeing your child—and I believe you should follow your heart. But childbirth changes people, and you may feel differently after the birth. I am only suggesting you give yourself permission to leave this option open. You may also want to consider if you want the adoptive parents with you when you say good-bye.

Whether or not you see your baby, you may want to also consider writing a letter at this time. Depending on your adoption arrangement and the level of openness, you may want to have something to give the adoptive parents that they can pass on to your child when he becomes old enough to ask questions about you. It may be a letter telling your child about you or telling him why you made the decision you did. Or you may just want to tell him how much you love him. It can be a very difficult letter to write—it was for me—but because your emotions are strong, it will show in your writing, and your child will someday treasure knowing how you felt about the day he was born.

Leaving a newborn at a hospital and walking away take enormous strength and conviction. The support of family and counselors during this time is critical. Emotions are overwhelming and can put a cloud over the goals. Discussions about the baby's future and the birthmother's continued role in it are essential in giving her the strength she needs. "It is their understanding that they will always know their children are in loving families, and may even remain part of their lives, that provides many with the impetus and the strength to proceed with their adoption plans" (Pertman).

Each birthmother will have her own personal barometer of how much contact she will want with her child, and these choices deserve respect. She's put her heart on the line to make a choice for someone else; it's time to let her make choices for herself. She may be happy; she may need to cry; she may want to hold her child; she may just want to look into his eyes. She may need company; she may need to be alone. Respect her choices during this journey, and she'll find her way through it.

My Joe

It was April 4, Good Friday, and true to the end, my family had gone on to mass without me. It had been months since I'd been to church, which was all right with me. I was convinced that the God that had helped me get through all this so far could not be in a building full of people who were unforgiving of my sins.

I sat in my dad's ugly red-orange recliner and watched the news. It was nice to be alone and be able to rub my belly without feeling self-conscious in front of my family. I was a full week overdue and had begun to accept the idea that I was going to be pregnant forever. Just before everyone returned, I felt a warm rush of liquid, as if I had peed in my pants. I was horribly embarrassed, even though I was completely alone, and I ran to the bathroom to clean myself up. After putting on fresh pants I returned to the living room, and it happened again. By the time my parents got home, I was sitting on the toilet "peeing" every ten to fifteen seconds. I had no idea that my water had broken—the first sign of labor. I thought that maybe the baby was just putting a lot of pressure on my bladder.

My mom stepped into action, slightly panicked, slightly excited, very worried. She talks fast when she's nervous (a trait I've inherited), and that night she had

plenty to say. Dad, on the other hand, went into the living room to watch TV. He was calm and quiet and mumbled something about how it would probably be hours yet before we had to do anything. He'd been through this four times already, and the calm his experience had given him flowed throughout our house. Everyone settled into a waiting routine.

At fifteen, my younger sister Karen thought it was all a game—literally. She got out a Trivial Pursuit game and kept firing questions at me to keep me busy. The youngest, Jane, hid upstairs most of the night, appearing only briefly when curiosity got the best of her. Karen got out a notebook and kept a nice record (in case anyone needed it) of each contraction, each fluid leak, and my general pain threshold. It didn't hurt yet at all, so it was almost fun. We laughed about the answers in the game and teased each other about the ones we didn't know. I learned that an aglet is that little plastic piece at the end of a shoelace, and we wondered if inventing something so small but functional had made the inventor rich. Growing up with next to nothing on our farm had led to an ongoing fantasy of wondering what it would be like to be rich, and we found ways to bring it into any conversation.

Sitting cross-legged on the floor in the doorway of our small bathroom, wavy red-brown hair falling off her shoulders and brushing against plump pink cheeks, Karen looked like a little fairy sitting in a buttercup waiting for spring to arrive. Her sparkling green eyes were wide with excitement and wonder as she asked if it hurt

and wondered if I should be on the toilet at all. What if the baby fell in the water?

I assured her that the baby would not simply fall out. The film I had seen in birthing class made it pretty clear I wouldn't be getting off so easy. I looked into the mirror across from where I was sitting and was surprised at how old I suddenly seemed to look. Playing the game with Karen, I felt inside as I did when we were little and hiding in forts in the hayloft giggling about nothing in particular and sharing secrets. But looking into the mirror I saw that my body had been defying my mind and had continued to grow up.

The last question Karen had asked me was: "Which insect has teeth—mosquitoes or fleas?" Neither of us was sure, and at that moment I was getting uncomfortable and really couldn't have cared less. "Who cares?" I barked at her. Then, seeing her hurt face, I quickly added, "So are you going to tell me or what?" She brightened immediately and answered that mosquitoes have wings and fleas have teeth. We laughed together briefly before another contraction hit, and I yelled for Mom.

After surveying Karen's chart and timing a couple of contractions herself while monitoring how hard my stomach felt, Mom deemed me ready to go. As with Dad, her experience of bringing four girls into this world gave her a sense of calm and control that allowed me to relax and put my trust in her.

Karen begged to go with us; she of course was immediately denied. It was almost midnight. Mom pointed out

that she had been lucky to be allowed to stay up this late in the first place. Besides, someone had to stay home with Jane. The mood began to change as we gathered my things and Dad closed the front door and headed for the car. I sat in the back, alone. It was very dark, and I stared out the window, not really seeing what was there but what I wanted to see. The new life of spring was just beneath the surface of the valley we lived in, waiting patiently to break through into the sunshine. I envied it. Once out, the green and the beauty would be there for all to enjoy for months. On the other hand, my baby, once out, would be gone in two days.

We drove into Dubuque, past the unforgiving church, past the rows of houses full of judging people and those we were lucky enough to fool. I could see inside some of the houses where the lights illuminated their contents. Most homes were dark, families asleep, content in their lives together and releasing the stress of their day. It'd be years before I could do that.

By the time we arrived at the emergency entrance to the hospital, I was a bit panicked because the contractions had started to hurt and come more often. I had been egging my dad on to drive faster. He stopped the car and turned back to hold my hand and said, "Don't worry, babe. I got a feeling this little guy's coming at five on the fifth!" He gave me one of those smiles that made the edges of my vision blur. For that one instant, I could believe, everything was okay.

Then I got out of the car. Mom put her arm around me. I looked over my shoulder and watched Dad drive away. "Is he coming in?" I asked Mom.

"No," she answered. "This is too hard for him. He's going home." One more pang of guilt before the contractions took over. Hurting my dad was more painful than any of the contractions I had had so far.

The big glass doors parted. Mom held my hand, and together we walked through.

I only vaguely remember entering the maternity ward, changing into a gown, getting onto the bed. What I do remember clearly is the butterfly. During our Lamaze classes they had told us to find a "focal point," something to concentrate on to distract us from the pain. The room I was in had a border near the ceiling with pastel colored butterflies. I remember thinking how nice it looked—sweet and cheery.

At three a.m. I hated that damn butterfly. I glared at it, daring it to flutter, to look happy, to blissfully fly away to a better place. I projected every ounce of pain I felt onto its back, and got pissed each time it was not crushed.

Between contractions, Mom gingerly offering me ice chips, and dozing in and out of consciousness, I made phone calls to Eric. I still thought of him as my soul mate and wanted to share everything with him. I needed him to be there. His roommate made excuses about his working late. After four in the morning I gave up. I found out later that he had spent the night with another girl.

A nurse came in and announced that it was time to move me. When she asked me to get up from the bed and crawl onto a gurney, I thought she was crazy. My insides were burning, every muscle was pushed past function,

and I was suppose to just hop up onto this bed as if I were at a track meet in high school? Somehow I did manage to get there. They put me in what looked like an operating room. My feet were yanked up into cold stirrups, and a large dome light was pulled over my body. I looked up at it and instantly was convinced I was dying. The light was so blinding I saw pure color and was sure that I had left my body.

The next contraction came and reminded me clearly that I had not. I closed my eyes and, between screams and squeezing my mother's hand into an unrecognizable form, tried to do as I was told. They had been asking me for awhile if I felt the need to push. I had no idea what I was suppose to be pushing with, so I answered no. Finally the doctor said it was time to push. The nurses told me to try. My mother urged me on. Not having a clue what I was suppose to do, I remembered a comment my dad made once about the sit-ups I was doing and pushing the baby out. So I did a sit up. When I contracted my stomach muscles, it felt so good I couldn't stop. I thought, "Oh my God! Why didn't they tell me to do this hours ago?" I kept my eyes closed, stopped breathing, and pushed with everything I had.

After some time I recall my mother screaming at me to breathe. All I could think was that if I stopped to breathe, the pain would come back, and there was no way in hell I wanted to feel that again. Finally, I had to breathe. I gulped for air as quickly as I could, eager to dive under again and push. By the third push my mother was screaming again. This time it was "Open your eyes!

Patty! Open your eyes!" I couldn't think of what she thought I should see. The damn butterfly was in the other room. "Open your eyes! It's your baby!" she screamed again. I opened my eyes.

Instantly I saw the reflection in the mirror above my knees. It was the top of an infant's head. I was so shocked that I couldn't move or breathe. He was real. *That's my baby*, I thought. *There really is a baby inside me.* It was surreal. Time stood still. The edges of my vision were blurred again.

Then the doctor looked me straight in the eye and said, "Give me one more good push, dear." I didn't want to close my eyes again. I tried to keep them open, but as soon as I started to push, I had stopped breathing again and had my eyes glued shut. Then a loud cry brought me back. I opened my eyes, and there he was. My son. "He's beautiful," Mom whispered in my ear as she hugged me. His long legs were kicking, and his tiny fists punched at the air trying to take down whoever it was that was holding him out in that cold, bright, light.

I couldn't take my eyes off him. The doctor handed him to the nurse, and she wrapped him in a blanket and carried him over to the corner of the room. Panic hit me as she turned from me. *Don't take him away yet!* I thought. Quietly, I asked the nurse if I could hold him. She looked at my mother for direction. "Of course you can," my mom answered. The nurse smiled and placed him in my arms.

The tears started to form and fall as I kissed him over and over and over, whispering the first of hundreds of "I

love you's." Mom was crying, too, and we both frantically wiped the tears away so they wouldn't cloud our vision. I don't remember if we said anything else to each other; I just remember that in that moment when I held my son, as my mother held me, we were a family.

Back in my room, as I held him in my arms, a nurse asked me if I had a name for him. She explained that the adoptive family would probably change it, but it would be okay if I wanted to give him a name until then. Nancy had already explained all of this to me months before. I told her his name was Joseph Paul. Joseph, because of the family nickname "Jo" that my cousin and I had been calling him for months. It was the only way to send a piece of me and my family with him. And Paul, after my friend who was the first and only one to say congratulations. I wanted Joseph to carry with him only the happiness from when he was in my womb. Paul had said having a child was a beautiful, wonderful thing, and he was right—it WAS wonderful.

She commented, "That's a nice name," and wrote it down on some chart. I wish I could remember the names of the nurses I encountered there, because their amazing kindness and understanding toward me during my time with Joe was unforgettable. I am eternally grateful for their cautious care and their understanding of what it was I needed in order to get through what was coming in two days. They always seemed to know what I needed— when I needed to see my son, when I needed time alone.

I spent hours holding Joe. I memorized his eyebrows. His toenails. Every wrinkle of skin. I found each part of his body that resembled mine or that of someone in my family. I mimicked his yawn, his cry. I was awed by his every move. The way he sucked on the knuckle of his thumb. The way his fist curled around the hem of my nightgown when he slept. The way his knees fell to the outside when he was asleep. I cherished everything about him, his crying when he was hungry, his soft snore when he slept, even the yellow streaks he made in his diaper. To this day I have a towel he spit up on in a box in my closet.

Scattered throughout my quest for knowledge of every detail about Joe were the moments I would just hold him and whisper "I love you." So our time together looked something like this: feel the softness of the tips of his fingers, say "I love you," smell his hair, say "I love you," listen to his breathing, say "I love you," measure his wrist between my thumb and finger, say "I love you." It was a steady routine, with the exception of the record skipping now and then as I repeated, "I love you, I love you, I love you. . . ."

Those who came to visit me were always upbeat and cheerful, cooing over how cute he was, bragging over his resemblance to their side of the family. My sister Karen was beyond amazed. She touched him softly and giggled when he moved and whacked her with his fist. I have photos of Grandma holding her first great-grandchild. My godmother holding her first great nephew. My mother

holding her first grandchild. And me holding my son. There isn't a single photo where you can see my entire face. In each one I am looking down at Joe. I couldn't take my eyes off him. I didn't want to miss a precious second of him. Because I knew that's what I had—seconds.

My father came to visit me, but he did not come in the room if he knew I had Joe. Mom told me that he did not want to know if it were a boy or a girl and he did not go to the nursery to see him. When he came to see me, he would ask how I felt and quickly change the subject to talk about something going on at home on the farm. Although it was hard, I respected his need to get through these days in his own way. He would be giving up his first grandson, and I fully understood all that it meant to him.

Eric came to visit, but I don't remember anything we said to each other. My best friend, Lori, came, and a few other friends who had not disappeared. My favorite time, though, was at night. At night there were no visitors. No one from the outside to bring reality in the door with them. It was just me and my Joe.

I would walk down to the nursery and stand at the window watching him. Eventually a nurse would notice me and ask if I would like to hold him. She already knew the answer. Back in my room I would cuddle him close, breathe him in, and sing softly the songs I had sung to him for months. I told him how much I loved him and focused on the moment—I wasn't ready for tomorrow yet.

On the second day I wrote a letter to Joe for his parents to give him when he was older, something Nancy had suggested I do. It was almost impossible to start. I stared at the paper a long time, baffled as to how I was going to put a lifetime of "I love you's" and "I'm sorry's" into one short letter. The "I love you's" came easily, pouring onto the paper, filling pages and pages. The rest left labor in the dust as the most painful experience of my life. I had to explain to him why I chose adoption. Again, the "I love you's" poured out. Writing a letter about how and why I gave him up for adoption before I had actually done it, when I was not even sure if I could do it, was like writing a prescription for unbearable pain.

I don't remember what I did write other than "I love you," but I remember that it took everything out of me to do so. I wrote a short letter to his parents, too, thanking them for giving my son all I could not, telling them I would pray for their family, and asking them to please let me know he was all right each year. It was very difficult to trust strangers, to ask them not to forget me. I understood I was asking a lot, especially from the adoptive mother. I prayed that God would help her to trust me too, that he would help all of us to do the right thing for my son.

That night, when I walked down the corridor to the nursery, I made it just to the stretch of window when my knees buckled and I fell to the floor. I vaguely remember a nurse helping me to get back to bed and telling me I should get my rest. I was so angry with my body. I did not want to rest—I wanted to see my son. I wanted more time.

The next day I got my wish. After hearing of my episode the night before, my doctor warned me that if it happened again he would have to keep me in the hospital another day. I thought, no problem! So as soon as he left, I made a dash for the nursery to repeat the event. Down I went, and an hour later Dr. Whalen gave me a precious gift—one more day with my son.

Later that day, when I was alone in my room, holding Joseph, a nun walked in. She told me to hand the baby over to her. Thinking she was some kind of volunteer there to help me and take the baby back to the nursery for me, I told her I wasn't done yet. She immediately launched into a tirade about what an awful person I was, that I had sinned and I had no right as a sinner to be selfish and hold the baby. She said that I was hurting him with my sin, that I would go to hell for what I had done. She kept insisting I hand him over!

I was so confused and shocked; I had no idea who this person was or how she knew anything about me. The staff at the hospital had all been so caring and kind. Who sent this person into my room to scream at me? Why was she calling me selfish? I was about to do the most UNselfish thing I had ever done in my life! I knew I had sinned when I had sex, but was this really the time and place to address it? All of this was racing through my mind, but mostly, my mothering instincts were kicking into full gear: she was yelling, and it was stressing out my baby! I was not about to let her hurt him!

I held Joseph close and pointed to the door, ordering her to get out. She continued her rampage for about a minute as I repeated "Get out! Get out! Get out!" in a growl that came from somewhere so deep inside me, I surprised myself.

She finally left, screaming something at me, but I didn't hear her anymore. I never did find out who she was. I leaned against the closed door holding Joseph close. I felt dizzy, and I couldn't catch my breath. At that moment Joseph made a soft cooing sound and looked straight into my eyes.

The world melted away. I was alone with my son, and he was looking at ME. It was as if he was saying, "It's okay, Mom. I love you." Somehow I made my way back to the bed and snuggled in with him. He grabbed at the neckline to my gown and held it tight in his tiny fist. "I don't want to let go either," I whispered, and held him closer. We sat there quietly looking at each other. I don't remember for how long. In my mind, it never ended. That moment, after I got to be his mom and protect him, and he got to be my baby and cling to me, is the one moment, the one snapshot in my heart that will exist for eternity.

The remainder of the day I cried. I held Joe. I prayed. I cried. I told him I loved him. I cried. I prayed that God would watch over him, that his new mother would love him as I did. Mom came, and we spent time together, crying, holding Joe, crying, telling him we loved him, and talking about his new family. Eventually a nurse took

him to the nursery so they could give me a final check up and I could shower and get ready to go home.

The next thing I knew I was standing in the hall outside of the nursery. It was time to say good-bye. I was swallowing back the tears, willing them to stay away. I would never forgive myself for blurring our last moments with tears and sobs. I wanted to see him clearly, hear him clearly, and remember every second of it. And I did.

I walked slowly into the small hallway next to the nursery. He was sleeping in his bassinet. The nurse smiled, her blue eyes reflecting the bright flowers of her smock. Her large soft hands rested on her wide hips, and her expression revealed the pain this scene was causing her as well. She told me it had been a joy to get to know me and a blessing to get to care for Joe while he was there. He was a perfect angel, she said. She pointed to a photo she had taken the day before of me holding Joe. She had taped it to the inside of the bassinet where Joe could see it. Then she handed me another photo she had taken just minutes earlier, saying she thought I would like it. I'll always be grateful for her thoughtfulness. But I didn't need a photo to remember. It's all clear as a bell, even today.

His head was turned to the right. His legs fell to each side, his feet touching at the heels creating a circle. His arms were up on each side of his head. His fists were pulled in tight with the thumbs on the outside. His breathing was soft and through his open mouth. He was absolutely beautiful.

I kissed his forehead, whispered "I love you" for the

last time into his left ear, touched his right hand softly with my fingertips, and turned to walk away. I made it two steps.

Just outside the nursery door, my knees buckled as the room started to sway. I grabbed at my mom, and looking at her, I saw two faces filled with pain and beginning to cloud with worry. A nurse came from behind me and scooped me up in a wheelchair. Once I sat down, my head cleared, and I whispered to the women who where clamoring to help me, "I'm okay." I was not even out of the hospital and had already begun lying about how I felt.

Mom made small chat with the nurse as she wheeled me down the hall. At the nurse's station I signed some papers and thanked them all for their help and care. Some had tears in their eyes. All of them were too overcome with emotion to speak. They just smiled weakly at me and nodded their heads. The nurse pushed me down the hall, into the elevator, and to the main floor. As we passed doors and people, my vision started to tunnel, and I felt the world around me growing tighter and closer. By the time we reached the main doors, all I saw was the back seat of our car where I was supposed to go next. I knew Dad was there in the front seat, but the perimeters of my vision were fading fast, and even the backseat was getting blurry.

While the tears had been escaping throughout our journey away from Joe, it wasn't until the hospital doors closed behind me that the sobs began. Grief folded in my vision completely now, and all I saw was my son lying in

his bed sucking his thumb, alone. I couldn't hold back anymore. The crying turned into full blown sobbing, and the tears were coming so fast I didn't even bother to wipe them anymore. We pulled in the driveway to our farm, and as the car came to a stop, Mom asked, "Are you okay?"

My crying stopped abruptly as I looked up. A new wave of emotion hit me as the anger washed over the grief, and I growled at her, "If feeling like your heart has just been ripped out with a chainsaw is 'okay,' then yeah, I'm feeling okay!" I jumped out of the car, raced up the sidewalk and into the house, past the wondering eyes of my little sisters, and up the stairs to my room, where I planned to remain until the end of time.

Chapter Five

Time to Heal

All too often, after a child is relinquished, those around the birthmother view the event as over. Nothing could be further from the truth. Regardless of the kind of adoption, birthmothers have fears that need to be addressed and respected. Many of these fears form from the grief process. Even though you are secure in your decision, you experience a loss. This loss affects everyone differently. Only you know its depths and what you need to work through it. Other members of the birth family feel this loss as well. It can be a confusing time as everyone tries to find a balance in their life again

This chapter will guide you through this process. While there is no one "right" answer to how to go through this, if you take the time to acknowledge your feelings, ask for what you need, and respect everyone's individual path through this loss, you will find your way. We will explore the following aspects of this time to heal.

- ◆ Time to grieve.
- ◆ Moving on.
- ◆ Birth family's grief.

♦   Finding closure for your decision.

Working through loss of any kind takes time. There is no reason to put time restraints on how long to heal. However, moving forward with your life and settling the questions and fears you have should be a priority. It is possible to still feel loss but begin to function in your everyday life and find your balance again.

Time to Grieve

No one expects you to drive home from the hospital, clear out the maternity clothes from your closet, put on a dress, and go out dancing. In the immediate hours after leaving your child, you will need to take the time and space you need to grieve. Let the feelings come out. Don't try to be the brave one—yet. Find a shoulder to cry on, or do an activity that gives you comfort. For me, it's baking. I remember when my grandmother died I baked enough food in one evening to feed all of my first cousins at the nursing home for two days—all eighty-four of them!

Some will tell you that there are a certain number of "stages" of grief and that you will go through each of them in order. Actually, theories about grief range from four to twelve stages, phases that overlap, or tasks you must accomplish. Don't worry about the theories. According to Howard Gorle, "humans are unique and cannot be forced into particular patterns of behavior." You will find your own way to journey through this.

Bev Swanson, author of *Wide My Ocean, Deep My Grief*, describes the grief process in this way:

The grieving process closely parallels a journey through the uncharted and very rough waters of a deep, deep ocean filled with unknowns. Waves of emotion are continually washing over you and sometimes it feels as though they will drown you. Other times the sun seems to come out as if to mock you. Suddenly you are once again washed over by terrifying waves of emotion tumbling you again into the depths of the cold icy waters. These depths at times feel so deep that you fear you will never find your way to the surface again.

But you will. Think of your loved ones and your counselors as your boat crew. They have the oxygen tanks, the life rafts, the life jackets, the rope lines to keep you connected. They WILL be there, even when you can't see them. They may be right outside your door just waiting for the chance to hug away your problems.

Your grief may elicit a variety of emotions: sadness, anger, frustration, guilt, shock, and numbness. You may feel physically fatigued or weak. You may begin behaviors that are unusual for you: loss of appetite, insomnia, retreating socially, crying, dreams, or nightmares (Gorle). If any of these emotions or behaviors seems to take hold of you and not let go, ask for help. You may feel like retreating to your room and never coming out or letting someone in, but don't act on those feelings. Let people help you. Be alone for periods of time when you really need to, but remember there are people who care about you and who are there for you (your counselor, for starters). Most adoption agencies offer post-adoption counseling, and most have birthmother support groups. Make some time to be with these people; they will help you to put one foot in front of the other.

Moving On

Placing your child for adoption is an event that will affect the rest of your life. You won't forget it. You will always remember the pain of the loss. But it is over. It is time to put it into your memories and not let it be the focus of your every day. In order to move ahead you may have questions you can't answer that make you feel stuck. Voice these thoughts to your support network, and let them help you find the answers. Here are some examples of the types of feelings and questions you may be asking yourself.

Am I the only one who understands how this feels?

If you are feeling that no one understands how you feel, you may be right. This is an experience unlike any other, and only others who have been through what you have will truly understand your pain. This doesn't mean other people cannot understand—everyone understands pain and loss. But it can be very comforting to talk with others who understand the specifics of your situation. This is one of the reasons I wrote this book. There are books that look at this issue from a medical or psychological point of view, and they can provide a lot of information and guidance. But I want you to know that there are other birthmothers out there who have felt the pain you feel—and survived. It's not a theory; it's not a wish or hope—it is real. I share very honestly with you in my story the emotions I experienced. I'm not going to pat you on the head and say, "It's okay." I know it's not. I know how much it hurts. But it will get better. You will go on with your life.

You will find happiness. Find other birthmothers to connect with—your counselor will be able to help you with this. It will bring you comfort and hope.

Will life ever be normal again?

It may take time, and it may never be exactly as it was before, but it will return to a sense of normalcy. It will be up to you to discover what "normal" will be. It is likely that this experience has changed you as a person. You probably have grown in maturity and focus. You may find you have ambitions you did not before. You may find you have lost your desire for things you once wanted. What is normal is the tendency to want your life back. This can be helpful—and harmful at the same time. It is good to feel like going back to work or school, to want to spend time with friends and family again. However, acknowledge to yourself that you have changed.

Use this opportunity to look at your life "before" and see what may not have been productive at that time. Returning to a bad relationship, for example, just for the sake of returning to your life "before," may not be a positive route for your future. I made this mistake, and I hope you can learn from it. If I have any regrets about adoption, it's that I didn't continue counseling after leaving the hospital. I had talked myself into believing that it was over and the way to fix my life was to get back everything I had before—good or bad. I believe that if I had continued to see Nancy, she would have helped me to sort the good and bad of my life before and to make new choices to get my life on a path toward success.

Will I feel this way forever?

No. Feelings always change, even when we don't want them to. However, you may get stuck in a rut. Depression is a normal reaction to a great loss. Again, this is a reason to continue seeing your counselor. You don't have to "snap out of it" overnight, but you should work on a plan with someone to work past it.

Am I dishonoring my child by moving forward with my life?

You may feel as though it is a tribute to your love for your child to stay sad. It may feel like a betrayal to be happy, to return to your usual activities. It's normal to feel this way, but it isn't true. Remember how part of your decision-making process was to look at your own life and how it would turn out, considering how to become someone your child could be proud of? This is your time to do this. It would be a dishonor to your child to make a decision so that both of your lives could turn out well, and then throw it away.

If you have made an arrangement for open adoption, you will continue to have contact with your child, and most likely you will meet again someday. Don't you owe it to your child to live the best life you can so when you do meet you will be the type of person she will want to get to know? Moving forward with your life does not mean leaving your child behind. She will grow along with you. Put her photo in your room. When you get new ones, put them up too. Your child is going to grow and change and live a full life. You deserve to do the same.

Will I ever have a family of my own?

While there is no way to predict this, I can tell you that there is no reason why you shouldn't. Falling in love, getting married, and having a child are all events that happen in their own time, in their own way. You won't be able to make it happen. If you try, which you might, you will probably be disappointed in the end. Don't worry about what is to come, and focus on being the best you that you can. When you love yourself, it will be easy for others to love you as well.

Looking for others to validate who you are or to provide for you what you want in your life is usually just a quick fix and not lasting. Again, in the next part of my story you'll read that these are mistakes I made. I know it's hard to wait for a family when you feel it's the missing piece in your life. But love cannot be controlled or manipulated. It is a natural feeling with its own time table and level of intensity. What you really want is not just someone to love you, and not just a child, but the love of your life and a child who exists because of this love. Settle for nothing less.

Birth Family's Grief

While you are finding your way through your own grief, your family is searching for their own way through as well. Just like you, family members need the respect to be able to grieve in their own way. This can be a confusing time for all family members, as they try to love and support one another yet find the opportunity to grieve. It is a delicate balancing act between two extremes: hanging on to the loss and letting go to move forward with life. Often family members and birthmothers become stuck in one end of the spectrum.

You may be able to help one another. You may have such different approaches to handling your grief that you need space from each other. While your first priority is to take care of yourself, it can be therapeutic to help someone else. It may feel good to step away from your own pain for awhile and focus on helping others with theirs.

As you will see in my story, my father and I had completely different routes for getting through this grief period. What you will learn later in the book is why. Not understanding another's actions can be difficult. Sometimes you will just need to trust that there are reasons you don't understand, and still respect what another person needs. Having someone who is acting very differently from you may be helpful. While I did not understand or agree with my father's actions, it did help me to move forward with my life. He gave me the kick in the butt that I needed to get up and move. At the time I was angry with him for it because I didn't understand it. But I did respect that it was his way of getting through those months.

Confirming Your Choice

For many, the question "Did I make the right choice?" plays loudly in their heart, and it can become difficult to focus on much else. If there is a planned exchange of information, or even a visit with the adoptive family, the period before that happens can be a time when fears nip at the certainty of a birthmother's decision. As with the time before the child's birth, during this time the support of loved ones and counselors is instrumental in helping a birthmother to move forward with her life, without regrets.

Most likely if you chose an open adoption arrangement, it was because you wanted to know your child was okay, you wanted some confirmation that his life went on, that he was loved. Waiting for this information can make you feel as if you jumped off a cliff. You feel you are falling, with no control, just waiting to land. You have no idea if, when you do land, it will be a safe landing or you will crash. You keep trying to imagine different scenarios. In some, your child is with a wonderful family, and they all love him and are happy together. In others, your child is ignored, or even hurt, and his family is indifferent to his arrival. It can start to drive you crazy wondering which it will be.

I understand these feelings—I had them myself—but I know more now than I did then. What I now know is that families waiting to adopt a child undergo a very extensive process. They have invested huge amounts of time in searching for a child. They want a child so much that they are willing to let strangers come into their home and evaluate everything about them, to share their financial information, and to open their hearts in counseling. This process costs them time, money, a host of stresses. They will endure pressures from family members and friends with opinions, they will encounter difficulties in making arrangements, and they will put every last hope on the line—for someone like you. They are putting all of their faith in a girl or a woman they have never met before to trust them enough to give them her child. This entire process feels like falling off a cliff for them too.

Trust them. Let your decision settle in your mind and heart, and trust them to care for your child. The day will come when you get your confirmation, whether it's a letter or a photo or getting to meet them again. It may be soon, or it may not be for a year or even longer. Even if it never does come, you need to learn to let the question go. Instead of questioning what your child's life is going to be like, begin to question your own. Find out what your purpose is—and go for it. Be proud of what you have done. I assure you that your child's adoptive parents are proud of you—and thankful. Reading books such as *Dear Birthmother* will show you the point of view of adoptive parents and illustrate their immense gratitude.

Adoptive families can help by understanding how important that first letter or contact is to the birthmother. Respect the birthmother's need to know that the child she lost has now found a home. Communicate this by letter or phone or even in person so everyone can begin the healing process. It is a crucial first step and one that requires a huge amount of trust between the adoptive parents and birthmothers. The birthmother took that first step of blind trust when she relinquished her child. The adoptive parents take their first step with the first communication after relinquishment. Then the two parties can come together on a foundation of trust, where a long lasting, successful relationship will be built with honesty, respect, and love.

PUSHING FORWARD

Two days after leaving the hospital, my dad took me to sign the adoption papers. We didn't talk. I didn't feel any new grief, but then again, I was so full of grief at the time that a little more wouldn't have made a difference anyway. I was constantly dizzy and began to see triple.

I was so dizzy that Dad had to help me up the stairs. He assumed I was just overcome with emotion. Actually, I was so confused about how I felt physically that I barely had a chance to think about what we were about to do. By the time we reached Nancy's office, I was seeing double and had a hard time knowing which of her four hands to shake. Dad sat me down, and Nancy went over the papers. I don't remember a word she said. My head was exploding, my ears were ringing, the room was spinning, and I just wanted to lie down. I couldn't think; I couldn't hear. Both my dad and Nancy looked at me with sad eyes, believing what they were seeing was a woman whose heart was filled with pain. I was in pain. But to be honest, it had nothing to do with my heart.

It came time to sign the papers, and I was seeing triple again. Nancy had to put my hand in the right place so I could sign. By now, everyone understood that I was sick, not heartbroken. Signing the papers that relinquished Joe was emotional, but I had said my good-byes,

and now I just wanted him to be able to go home. I was actually a bit angry, because Brad had refused to sign the relinquishment papers. He didn't want to put his name to anything just in case I changed my mind and kept Joe. Nancy had tried her best to reason with him, but he wouldn't budge.

This meant that Joe would have to go to a foster home for two weeks. Technically during this time Brad could come and take him, since he hadn't given up his parental rights. After the two weeks the court would take his rights away. Then Joe would be free to be taken home by his new parents. I wasn't worried about Brad coming to get Joe—it was pretty obvious by now that he wanted nothing to do with him—but I was furious with him for taking those two weeks from Joe and his parents. I knew how important those first days were for bonding. It was bad enough Brad wouldn't step up and be involved in the pregnancy and my decision, but now his actions were hurting Joe. That was something I could never forgive him for.

After I signed the papers, Dad took me to the doctor's office. My vision was completely screwed up, and I could barely stand. I was having an allergic reaction to the drug they had given me to suppress milk production. They took me off the drug, and the next day I woke up with a clear head, a shattered heart, and a set of DD breasts that leaked.

It was over. Now what? My instincts told me what to do: get a job, get my own apartment, move on. But it was impossible to move any issue into priority number one in

my brain. Getting the first letter from Joe's parents, finding out that he was okay, knowing I had made the right choice—these were my priorities. I was content to simply sit on my parents couch and wait for the day the answers would come.

My father, however, had other ideas. The day after I signed the papers, I was sitting on our couch, settling in for the long haul, when Dad came in the kitchen door and hollered into the living room, "What are you doing in there?"

"Nothing," I answered.

"There's no time for 'nothing' around here. Get up and put on your boots. I need some help outside." I heard the screen door slam and knew no reply was requested.

I heaved a sigh and pulled myself from the couch, dragging my feet to the door. I stuffed them into my boots and followed his lead, letting the screen door slam behind me. Dad was in the horse pasture by a pile of old machinery that had been growing an interesting array of rust and weeds in it since we had bought the farm fifteen years earlier, his sea green pickup truck "Old Blue" next to it.

"Help me throw this stuff in the back of Blue," he said.

I was shocked. That junk had managed to grow there for fifteen years, and he never cared before. Why were we cleaning it up now? But I knew better than to question him, so I grabbed an old tailpipe and tossed it into the back of Blue with a clang.

A few minutes later, I told Dad that I wondered what my baby was doing at that time. He stopped cold, looked up at me, and said, "What in God's name are you thinking about that for?"

"Because I miss him," I answered.

"He's fine," Dad said. "It's time you forget about all that and start thinking about your future. Have you decided where you're going to apply for a job?"

And just like that, the door was closed. No looking back would be allowed in front of Dad—only discussions pertaining to the future.

Over the next week, if Dad caught me crying, he would instantly come up with a large job that had to be taken care of immediately, usually involving heavy manual labor. As Dad had always used hard work as a punishment, the significance of the chores was not lost on me. The punishment for not forgetting what I had gone through was working so hard that I couldn't think about anything except how physically exhausted I was.

Anyone who dared to start a conversation about Joe was quickly cut off. We already knew not to use his name around Dad, and we quickly discovered it wasn't even acceptable to discuss my recovery. My breasts fairly exploded for days, but if I complained, I was just told to suck it up and go do some chores to get my mind off it.

No one understood it. Mom said the pain was just too much for him and that he wasn't talking about it, even to her. I thought that was incredibly unfair. His loss! What about my loss? Why couldn't I be allowed to deal with my own loss in the way I wanted to? I was incredibly angry

with him. I was also hurt that for the first time ever, I was not able to share my feelings openly with my dad.

When the pictures from the hospital were developed, Dad ordered me to put them away. Mom, my sisters, and I had to look them over when Dad went out to do chores. Secretly we would share hugs, looks, small comments, and tears. When Dad walked through the door, everyone would put on their happy faces and pretend through the rest of the day. Dad made it very clear: I was to get over it, pick up my life and get it back on track, and never look back.

I thought my dad had lost all feeling. The man I thought felt love and compassion deeper than anyone I had ever known before I now felt was full of emptiness and anger. Mom tried to make me understand that the situation was just as painful for Dad, but all I saw was that he no longer had respect for my feelings. It was his way or no way, and I couldn't live with that.

Dad being negative didn't make any sense to me. My dad was the one who always made the hard stuff fun. He found joy in everything. He turned pulling weeds in the garden into a race and danced with the pitchfork while shoveling manure in the cow barn. I had counted on him to be the one to find the joy in giving Joe a new home. Instead he was pushing me to skip it completely. He was only interested in what I did—when would I find a job, when would I move out. I couldn't believe he wasn't doing anything—no races, no songs, no joy.

Getting angry with him fueled my search for a new job. Getting a job meant having the money to move out. I

couldn't stand to be near him. The father I had leaned on for months suddenly became a cold tyrant I didn't recognize. I spent full days out searching, and every night at dinner he would ask for a report of where I went and what I accomplished. If I had a day where I didn't go out or only went a couple of places, I'd get an ear-full. It was never enough for him. He pushed and pushed and pushed. He pushed until I got a job. He pushed until I got an apartment. He pushed until the tears stopped. Despite my determination to wallow in pain, I pieced together a new life and began to live again. The day I moved out was the first time I had seen him smile in months. At the time I thought he was just glad to get rid of me. It would be years before I understood his real motivation.

Looking back, I'm glad he acted as he did. If not for Dad's pushing, it probably would have taken years for me to accomplish what I did in a few months. I always knew I was too motivated to sit around wallowing in pain forever, but I definitely was interested in doing it for as long as I could at that time. Sometimes wrapping yourself in pain and withdrawing from the world begin to feel comfortable. It's hard to face people and situations. Hiding becomes the easy thing. It can become so comfortable and so easy that you never come out of it. Thanks to my dad, I did.

What really made me angry with Dad was that by appearing as if he didn't care about Joseph, he was missing out on loving him. Giving birth was such a profound experience for me. It was impossible to imagine someone not wanting to celebrate it, even if only for a short while. I

tried my best to understand his grief. I imagined it was simply too painful for him to face. I thought that after trying four times for a son and settling for four daughters, he found having to give away the first boy who finally entered our family was more than he could bear. On the other hand, wasn't it something to get excited about as well?

We had a boy! He may not be going to grow up with us, but he will always carry a part of us with him. I couldn't understand why Dad wouldn't want to know if Joseph was anything like him. I got caught between my anger at not understanding his motives and my sympathy that he was missing out on something big. These conflicts in my feelings would pull our relationship in many directions for years. It's sad to me now how we lost all those years, but at the same time I can't say that my life would have progressed the way it did if we hadn't gone through this. Being angry with my dad was the motivator that got my life back on track. While I was never sure what it was he wanted or needed, he always seemed very sure of what I needed.

I got a great job doing typesetting for the local newspaper. I loved being back around presses and light tables, and the daily pressure to meet the deadline was exhilarating. I loved the last minute rushing around to get the paper "to bed." I worked in a room full of men at least thirty years older than I, with the exception of one other woman. They were an entertaining group and loved to tease me about being so young. They took me under their wing and taught me the tricks of their trade. Those were

the days when a layout artist became an apprentice first, when you used black tape so thin it was nearly impossible to hold when putting a box around the copy or underlining a word in the text. The most important tool to have nearby was an impeccably sharp Exacto Knife. We worked at light tables and cut and pasted and drew and taped until the page was perfect. I loved every minute of it.

The next big change I made was buying my first car. It was a piece of junk—an orange Vega that leaked oil like a sieve and had a hole so big in the floor boards that my friends quickly dubbed it the "Flintstones Car." At one point I could only get it started if I used a screwdriver on the starter. But it was mine. I still preferred the bike, but now I had transportation for when it rained. Yay!

I got an apartment with a new friend, down in the old part of town on one of the longest streets in Dubuque. It was long, flat, straight, filled with small houses that all looked the same and a couple of churches and schools that looked as if they should have been condemned fifty years ago. If you followed it to its end, you ended up at the dam on the Mississippi, just below Eagle Point Park. For a small town we had one of the biggest and coolest parks I had ever been to. I loved to ride my bike down to the dam; there's something incredible about standing on the edge of a wall that's holding back the mighty Mississippi River. You realize how small your part is in this world, yet looking at the bricks in the wall, you see that it takes each of those

small parts working together to do something wonderful and grand.

That wall made me think of Joe. It took my family, me, Nancy, and Joe's adoptive parents working together on the same goal to make something wonderful happen. I knew my family, Nancy, and I had done our part. I hoped and prayed Joe's new parents would do theirs. I knew so little about them. I was going completely on instinct when I chose them. I was dying to get that first letter from them. I wanted to know; I needed to know: Do they love him as much I as do? I needed to see pictures—was he happy? Nancy had warned me that I might not even get a picture. I wasn't sure what to expect, but I knew I wouldn't be able to breathe clearly until I got that letter.

I attended a couple of birthmother meetings and grew terrified as others told of being promised letters or photos and never receiving them. The few who did get a picture after the first year never heard from their baby's family again. I quit going to the meetings. And I prayed.

Nancy had made it clear I wouldn't get the letter until Joe's first birthday in April 1986. I wasn't even sure if it would come directly to me or to Catholic Charities. Still, I ran to my mailbox every day. I had given Nancy my new address a week before I actually moved, just to be sure I wouldn't miss anything.

Despite the desire to stand by my mailbox for the next year, I managed to get into a nice routine. I worked every day, I hung out with my friends at night. Eric and I even got back together.

After Joe was born, we spent more and more time together, and in a short amount of time it was as if the previous year had not even happened. If Joe had been his baby, everything would have been different. It was difficult to think about, much less talk about, so Eric joined my dad and insisted we put it behind us and move on.

While I would someday understand my dad's actions as being motivated by love, I cannot say the same for Eric. I was so desperate at the time to get my life back to what I thought "normal" was (which included Eric) that I never took the time to see how Eric had turned things around on me. I didn't take the time to remember how he had been unfaithful to our relationship, that the idea of Joe being "ours" wasn't even a possibility, as we had long since parted. I was so busy trying to get everything in my life "before" back again that I forgot that maybe I didn't really want everything (especially him!) back again.

My roommate didn't last long, and soon I was alone. It was liberating to be on my own, but lonely and expensive. I got a new kitten from a woman I worked with at the paper. She was supposed to be a long-haired silver Persian, but apparently my friend's cat was playing the field because Putty (as in "I taught I taw a Putty-Tat!") turned out to be a short-haired, tiger-striped gray kitten. But I loved her. I could tell her all the things I was feeling that my dad and Eric didn't want to hear. She'd lick up my tears and rub against my cheek and play with my hair until my smile returned.

Putty also became a great alarm clock. Having to pay all the rent myself, I needed more income, so I took on

extra jobs. I did telemarketing calls to sell our local hockey team's coupon book, did freelance design work for local businesses, and when that wasn't enough, took a job as a waitress at Perkins. After a few months they offered me the full-time night shift. It was good money, so I couldn't turn it down. This meant working 7:00 to 3:30 at the paper, going home for two hours of sleep, then to work at Perkins from 8 p.m. till 4 a.m., going home for an hour of sleep in the bathtub (my idea of multi-tasking), then back to the paper. Sunday was my only day off, and I usually slept the entire day. Putty was great at nipping on my chin until I woke up—the two alarm clocks I had didn't always do the job, and even when they did I had to depend on the little red "p.m./a.m." light to know which job I had to get dressed for. Twice I showed up at Perkins in uniform only to realize it was morning, so I ended up having to work all day at the paper in my ugly yellow and orange bibbed dress.

Eric got a job in Des Moines and moved away, although we still considered ourselves a couple. I was so busy working I didn't have time to think. Every time I sat still, I fell asleep. Neither boss was very happy about how tired I was, but it was the first time I could remember that all my bills were paid and I even had money in a savings account.

I slowly pulled out of my social life. Sleep was just a higher priority. Lori wasn't very happy with me for getting back together with Eric, and while she was there when I needed to talk about Joe, she backed off when the topic of Eric came up.

I've always regretted not listening to her advice during this time. She was like my own personal Jiminy Cricket—the voice of conscience. But, like Pinocchio, I ignored the voice of reason and went with what felt good, until I learned my lesson.

Clinging to Eric, even after he moved away, was my way to fight to get my "before" back. Waiting for a letter from Joe's parents was emotionally draining; doubts and fears began to slip in. I had no control over his life now. The only life I had some control of was my own. Since I couldn't see the future anymore, I tried my best to reclaim the past, and that meant being with Eric. I realize now that our relationship was mostly in my head. In reality we only spoke on the phone once a week and he would come home to visit once a month—usually spending the bulk of time with his family or friends, not me.

However, the fantasy was working for me at the time, and since I was either working or sleeping most of the day, I didn't spend much time thinking about it anyway. I got into a routine, part of which was praying every morning that a letter would arrive that day.

Finally, in November, the first letter came. I didn't have to wait the full year after all.

Nancy called and said I could come to her office to get it. I was so anxious to read the letter that I don't remember what we talked about. Nancy was surprised and excited that the envelope contained fourteen photos and two letters—one from Joe's adoptive mother and one from his father. She made a point to tell me how unusual this was. Sharing information was a new idea for adoptive

parents then, and although many said they were open to it, often they did not follow through, and the birthmother ended up with nothing. Nancy was very excited that this time, just maybe, the adoptive parents would embrace the idea of an open relationship over the years.

I took the thick brown envelope and ran down the stairs, out the door, and across the lawn of the Catholic Charities building to a grove of trees. I sat down and cried while hugging the envelope, then forced the tears aside so I could clearly view my treasure.

I tore open the envelope and poured out the contents, the photos of my happy, beautiful, smiling son scattering about my lap like fallen leaves. I caught my breath. I couldn't move. I just looked. It was one of those perfect fall days where the air had only a slight chill in it that felt refreshing, not cold. The grove of trees I sat under was ablaze in orange, yellow, and red, the deep green of the late summer grass speckled with splashes of colors like a Monet painting.

Slowly I picked the photos up, feeling as though I were peeking into someone's window as I looked carefully at each one. There was one in which he was lying on the blanket I had given him. In all the pictures he had on adorable outfits. He was either smiling or sleeping, always with a soft snuggly blanket. There was one photo of him in a car seat, and one near a beautiful cat on a couch. He was home. He had parents who kept him safe, warm, and happy, and he showed the contentment all babies do when they are dearly loved. He even had a pet who loved him.

Because I Loved You

I opened the letter from his mother and began to read. The love and thankfulness she felt filled the pages. Her appreciation for what I had given her was overwhelming. Her respect for each of our parts in Joseph's life was undeniable.

I had only three gifts I could give Joe in the hospital: my love, a name, and one more day. The only one that I knew could be taken away was his name. In this first letter to me, his mother wrote of their immense sense of gratitude and gave me a gift: they named him Joseph Paul. They knew I must have chosen it for special reasons, and it was the only way that they knew of to honor me. He wasn't just my Joe anymore. He was their Joe too.

They had no delusions of erasing Joe's past and having his life begin the day he arrived at their house. By keeping the name I had given him they acknowledged that his life began with me. He may have been with me for only three days, but his life had already begun—and I most certainly had been a part of it. This level of respect for my part in Joseph's life was the first step in what would become a trusting, mutually respectful relationship. Joe's mother said in the letter that "children are never really ours—they are just entrusted to us for a time by God." They recognized that I had had my time, and it was now theirs, but ultimately Joseph was a child of God. Joseph was his own person with an entire life ahead of him, and we were all to count our blessings for being able to share a portion of it with him—that was the message I got from them.

Their letters conveyed respect, gratefulness, and most particularly, love. I could not have asked for more. They were everything I had hoped for and more. My son was loved. He was in a happy, loving, Christian home with two parents who loved each other, loved him, loved God, and loved me for my sacrifice. I had always known they had a home to provide him, incomes to support his needs, and each other to give him both a mother and a father in his life. The only question was if they would love him as I had thought only I could. After reading their letters I had not one doubt left in my heart that they most certainly did love their son, as only a true parent can.

After I had dried my tears (again), I carefully returned the letters and photos to their envelope, tucked it inside my jacket, and rode my motorcycle straight to my parents' house.

It was a Saturday afternoon, and Mom and my sisters Karen and Jane were all home. Dad was out of town on a jobsite. We gathered at the kitchen table, and I poured the contents of the envelope out. We cried together, we laughed together, and everyone sat breathless while I read the letters aloud. Amid tears Mom said simply, "Our boy made his way home."

Karen ran upstairs for a minute and returned proudly carrying a large shoebox. She had covered it with floral wrapping paper. "This is for you to keep all of your special memories of Joe in, so they'll be safe," she said. She carefully placed it in my hands as though handing me a crystal case. I gave her a hug and thanked her for all she had done for me. I returned the photos and letters

to their now worn brown envelope once more and gently placed them in the Box. I hugged everyone goodbye, wrapped the Box into my jacket, got back on my bike and drove off.

The entire last year of my life was spent waiting for this day. Now that it had come, I felt lost. There was no purpose left to my day. The more I looked at the photos and read the letters, the more I longed for what I had let go—a family. Joe had found his "happily ever after." Was I ever going to find mine?

Chapter Six

Finding Your Happy Ending

The decision for adoption is based on doing what is best for the child and the birthmother. So finding out the child is safe and loved is only half of the puzzle. What about the birthmother? Will she too find happiness? A family? Love? Searching for the answers to these questions will take many paths. The time it takes to truly recover from the experience of relinquishment varies from one individual to another. Other members of the birth family will have lingering effects of the experience as well.

Birthmothers and their families may believe that if they are moving forward with their lives, this automatically equates with putting the effects of the relinquishment behind. However, traumatic events can have subtle but lasting effects. You may not even realize you are still recovering from this trauma. You may know it but be unsure how to do anything about it. Recognizing some of the destructive paths may help to get you on the right road. This chapter will look at some of the effects of the trauma of relinquishment:

- ♦ Trying to go back.
- ♦ Trying to fast forward.
- ♦ Trying to replace the pain with another child.

We will also look at the steps you can take to move toward healing:

- ♦ Finding your true self again.
- ♦ Rebuilding relationships with your family.

As with each stage of this process, the guidance of a trained counselor could help you get through your recovery with as little damage to your life as possible. Personally, I skipped out on doing any real work on my recovery. When I finally made it through, and regained my strength and self-confidence, I found myself in the middle of a mess. I finally realized that I had some issues to face and some truths to discover before I could truly move forward. I hope that by sharing some of my mistakes I can help you avoid them. If you do find yourself falling into some of these routines, just know that they are very common. Don't blame yourself, but change your behavior if you can.

I found in doing research for this book that I was not alone. It is very common for birthmothers to follow the same paths that my life did. Some go through these stages quickly; others get lost in them for years. The lucky ones get through it with little or no additional damage to their lives. We're all searching for our own happy ending. We get lost when we try to find it—rather than letting it find us.

Trying to Go Back

One of the more common reactions to relinquishment for birthmothers is to try to regain their "before." You may see the period before finding out you were pregnant as what's "normal" for your life and try hard to go back there. In doing so, you may be denying your true feelings, even denying facts about how your life has changed. You may prefer to avoid the grief by rewinding your life to the time when it was not there. The danger here is that even though you may be able to avoid experiencing your grief, and live in denial for years, eventually it will catch up with you. The eruption of feelings later on may be more destructive to your life than if you face them right away.

You may feel pressured by others to forget what has happened, put it behind you, and move on. It's important you understand—and make others understand—that this is a false conception. Many researchers have disproved it. Adoption can feel like an amputation for some, where the birthmother still feels the child as being connected to her. Often, instead of a birthmother's pain disappearing, the need for information remains constant or increases. (Fravel, McRoy, and Grotevant).

One of the potentially harmful paths is returning to unsuccessful, even hurtful relationships. This may be with someone you knew before you got pregnant, back when you had a completely different outlook on your future. You may struggle to bring back that time and place through that person. But life moves on—for everyone. Entering a relationship based on the sole fact that the person was once a part of your past is not realistic.

Another way birthmothers try to "go back" is by marrying the birthfather of their child. You may fantasize that if you build a life together, you will then someday be able to have another child, and then you can finally become the family that you were not able to be at this point. Again, this is unrealistic. It is a huge burden to a relationship to have its future plotted out in such detail. Love, marriage, children—they have their own timing when they are right. When they are forced, it is a recipe for disaster.

Merry Bloch Jones found this as she interviewed birthmothers: "Birthmothers who married birthfathers fantasized about the relationship to the point of causing its end." Relationships need to be based on truths, facts, the reality of today, and the myriad of possibilities for the future. By forcing your relationship to be exactly as it was before, and to proceed exactly as you are envisioning, you are setting yourself up for disappointment and heartbreak.

Trying to Fast Forward

Another path, equally destructive as trying to go back, is to try to fast forward. Many birthmothers attempt to skip the grieving period by getting married. You may feel that if you can just create a new family, then you won't have to grieve for the one you gave away. This push to have a family often replaces previous goals and ambitions of careers or school. But if you follow this route, eventually you may find you are in a relationship that isn't working and living a life that is not what you had envisioned.

After realizing their mistake of using marriage as an escape from grief, women are faced with either staying in a loveless marriage or getting divorced. Neither is a happy option. In interviewing birthmothers who found themselves in this situation, Jones reports, "Those who pretended to be 'normal' or happy often found that their ability to keep up appearances soon wore thin." Most often these women became actors playing the part of wife while actually feeling very disconnected from their spouses. As Jones writes, "Dividing themselves and acting out roles that did not feel real usually took its toll on birthmothers. ... Most could not sustain the strain indefinitely and eventually sought relief through divorce."

Now the birthmother is faced with dealing with the grief of relinquishment and the grief of the end of a marriage. This can be a very confusing time. It can feel as though you are watching your life from the outside, instead of being a part of it. You set up these circumstances believing it was the right route to take, and in the end it took directions you couldn't control, and you feel powerless to change.

Your life may begin to get out of control. Then again, these events may be what bring you to face your grief head on so that you can get that control back. It can be very difficult to be strong and to make the right choices—and no one should have to do this alone. Dealing with grief from one event is hard enough, but from two it can be completely overwhelming. If you haven't had counseling before, now is the time to get it. Having someone to help you separate what is real and what is your vision through grief can help you to see the way out.

Trying to Replace the Pain with Another Child

Usually a part of the package of replacing the grief with a marriage is to replace the lost child with another. You try to get back all the good you felt in being a mother, carrying a child to term, giving birth, holding him, loving him.

But children can never be replaced. Each one is special in his or her own right. Each pregnancy will be different, and so will each delivery, each child. What you will learn if you have more than one child is that a mother's love is not about loving any child, it is about loving that child. You will love each child with the same intensity of emotion. Loving one will not eclipse the love of another. If you are grieving over a lost child, those emotions are connected to that child specifically. Another child will have no power to take grief and loss away.

This lingering emotion can have a tremendous impact on your ability to mother other children. Fears of losing the child are usually most profound. Separation anxiety is common between birthmothers and the children they have later. These fears may be mild and easily overcome, or they may be so fierce that they become inhibiting. If this occurs, it is important to seek help before it can have a negative effect on the child. It is never fair to place on a child the responsibility of calming a mother's fear.

Finding Your True Self Again

Open adoption has done much to help birthmothers to move forward through their grief and go on with their

158

lives. Knowing where your child is, that he has a loving home, provides peace. This peace of mind liberates the birthmother from many fears around her choice and does so much for helping her to heal and move on.

While semi-open adoption does allow for an exchange of information, this information is usually only exchanged on a yearly basis. This can often delay the birthmother's ability to find peace. The first year of waiting for information is usually the toughest. Even after the first letter confirming the child's life is full of happiness and love, a birthmother may have lingering doubts and fears. It only took six letters from my son's parents before I truly started to heal and find myself again. However, since these letters only came annually, it took me six years to really start to get through my grief. It was during this time that I made the most mistakes.

In a fully open adoption arrangement it is more likely that the birthmother will get the confirmation she needs in a more timely manner and thus find her peace sooner. If you are considering a semi-open arrangement, it's important to discuss with your counselor the possibility of more frequent communications, at least in the beginning.

When you cannot find your peace through communication with the adoptive family, then it is important to discover other ways to deal with your grief. Jones found that "more than any other single source, the support they found the most effective came from other birthmothers."

However you find your way, give yourself permission to go through this process. Don't try to skip it in any way. You will not be the same person when you come through it—most likely you will be stronger. Work at loving yourself again, being strong, building your confidence, becoming independent. When you have met your needs and dealt with your feelings and your grief, you will then be able to give of yourself to others. And your happy ending will come.

Rebuilding Relationships with Your Family

Grief over a lost child is not exclusive to birthmothers. Birth families go through these stages as well. Everyone will have a grief process to follow. Everyone's life will be affected. For my parents, the emotional drain and tremendous weight of parental responsibility left them searching for happiness again. Dad bought a new motorcycle, and he and Mom took long cross-country trips on it. Unfortunately, this meant often leaving my youngest sister, Jane, to fend for herself during her high school years. I felt guilty for this and tried my best to spend extra time with Jane, especially if Mom and Dad were on one of their trips. My sister Karen saw for the first time that life has many possibilities.

Growing up during the time we did and where we did, we believed our lives were already mapped out: meet a boy, get married, have a family. Pick a job, work hard at it, retire. We all began to see how unrealistic this was. The positive side was that we were less afraid of change. Karen and Jane were both more open to taking chances on new paths in their lives. For each of them, it meant not being afraid to move from our hometown, change careers until they found the right one for them, and not fall for the first guy who's nice but hold out for true love. Because Sue was overseas with the Navy all this time, she was the least affected, but she was sorrowful at the loss of a family member nonetheless.

My parents never did get more comfortable discussing sex with us girls. They had been brought up to consider it taboo to speak of, and it was a hard habit to break. However, my sisters and I now felt the need to discuss every aspect of sexual activity. We often shocked my mom with our frank conversations. While she didn't often participate, she didn't stop us either. All of us girls vowed to tell our own children the truths about sexual activity before they even had their first crush.

The closer to the birthmother and her child each person is, the more he or she will be affected. Just as it was important for the birthmother to face her grief and not try to avoid it, birth families need to do the same. Communication among family members is often the best route for getting everyone on track to heal. Use this experience to grow closer, not to pull apart. Be there for each other. Think of the feelings other family members may have—sometimes helping them with theirs is exactly what you need to get you through yours. For years I had no idea the depths of the fears my father had been living with—until the day he called me up and said, "Bring the Box."

SEARCHING FOR A FAIRY TALE

For a year I had lived with the fear that I had chosen the wrong family for Joe, but once that fear had been put to rest a new fear slowly emerged: would I ever find a family of my own? Without realizing it, I became desperate to find love and to create a family.

I moved to Des Moines to be closer to Eric and began to seriously pressure him about marriage, only to find once again that he would rather explore his choices a while longer than be tied down. I finally accepted that I couldn't go back. I couldn't just blink and pretend the last year never happened. I decided to move back to Dubuque and start again.

I became convinced that what I really needed in order to heal was to replace what I lost: a family. I spent a year auditioning men for the part of father and husband. On the first date I would analyze their potential and make a decision. I'd kiss any frog I could find, and when he didn't instantly become my prince, I'd leave. Instead of getting to know someone and having a real relationship, I was looking for a fairy-tale ending.

In the fall of 1987, I found my prince. Nicholas was from England, very sure of himself, and more than willing

to sweep me off my feet and make me feel as though I would never have to worry about another thing as long as I lived.

After dating me for just two months, he took me to England and, on the corner between Big Ben and West-minster Abbey, proposed. The little farm girl from Iowa had stepped into her fairy tale.

While I thought my dreams were all finally coming true, my best friend, Lori, thought it was all a nightmare. I thought Nicholas was the answer to my prayers. I was tired of doing my own thinking; I didn't trust my decisions anymore, and I was happy to let him take care of me. She saw him as overbearing and controlling, turning me into a passive follower she didn't recognize. Lori was so disappointed in the direction I was taking my life that she ended our friendship.

The next summer, Nicholas got a job in Madison, Wisconsin, and so we moved there. We were married in the fall of 1988, and just over a year later, the week of Joe's fifth birthday, my dream became complete when I realized I was pregnant. Nicholas was furious when, as I had each year since his birth, I took off work on the day of Joe's birthday to look at the contents of the Box and remember. With a new baby on the way, he felt it was time to let Joe go. I had thought a new baby would make me forget, too, but instead I thought of Joe more than ever.

Rachel was born on October 3, 1990. Giving birth to her brought back so many memories and fears that I only vaguely remember Nicholas being a part of it. What I do

remember is the moment they said we could go home. I felt as if I were stealing a baby. I was convinced that at any moment someone would jump out to stop us and take her away.

My paranoia grew over the coming days. I never let her out of my sight. I held her twenty-four hours a day. I woke up screaming in the night after nightmares that Nancy was at our door saying, "Don't you remember? You agreed to give us all your babies." After a week of this Nicholas called my mother. It took her two days to get me to get up off the couch, let her hold Rachel, and take a shower.

My fear of losing Rachel slowly ebbed with time, but it never went away completely. For years, if we were shopping and she got out of my sight for even a second, I would scream her name so loudly that everyone around us became convinced that I had escaped from some mental facility. She's learned over the years to always tell me where she will be, but I still begin to panic if I can't find her at her track meet or basketball game.

Just after Rachel's first birthday, we took a trip to help out my parents. They had recently moved to Cassville, Wisconsin, and were building a campground in the valley that overlooked the Mississippi. Dad called and simply said, "Bring the Box." Since the subject of Joe was strictly forbidden by my father, I was shocked that he even knew the Box existed.

The Box my sister had made for those first letters from Joe's family now contained six years' worth of letters and pictures, his birth certificate, the account of my

contractions that Karen had kept, and a white burp towel from the hospital that still had a yellow stain from where he had spit up on it.

I brought the Box, and we met in his workshop. I was ready to defend remembering. I was ready to defend grieving. I was ready to defend feeling. I was not ready to see my father cry.

Dad busied himself with something at the workbench, his hands stained from years of grease and grime and hard work for his family. He had his back to me and didn't talk for a long while. When he turned, there were tears in his eyes. When I was sixteen, Dad had an emergency appendicitis. After witnessing my father cry for the first time that day in the hospital, I had become convinced that if I ever had appendicitis, it would kill me. So when I saw that my father was crying again, I knew without a doubt that whatever he was about to do or say, it would be big. And I was sure it would kill me.

As Dad began to speak, the weight he had carried for six years began to lift, and what I had thought was hardness in his face I began to recognize as determination and protection. That night my father told me about his mother and how she had quit living when his father passed away at a young age. He cried as he told me about how vital and alive my grandmother had been when he was young, how she was always full of happiness and love and adventure. I didn't recognize the person he was describing. My memories of Grandma were all of her being on the verge of dying. For the twenty-three years I knew her, she rarely smiled, had little to say, and

was in the hospital more than out. She never seemed to be actually diagnosed with anything, although she insisted she was dying.

Dad said that when I decided to give up Joe, he was afraid I would do the same, and that was why he pushed me so hard. He had to suppress his own need to grieve in order to help me get past mine. Now that I had my own business again, a family, and another child, he was sure I had made it through. His pent-up grief finally came pouring out, and, for the first time, he asked to see a picture of his oldest grandchild.

After Dad's confession, I took a hard look at the past six years. I felt immense guilt for my anger I had held toward him, and shame for being so selfish to have only been concerned with my own grief. I had thought Dad had banned my grieving in order to fulfill his need to grieve, when just the opposite was true. Dad had denied himself a chance to grieve in order to help fulfill my need to move on with my life. I began to question whether or not anything had been as it seemed for the past six years.

I started frantically searching for more missing pieces and more answers. I called Eric. I called Nancy. I called Lori. I re-lived the loss. I reexamined how I felt about my marriage and about Rachel's birth.

Slowly, I discovered that instead of becoming whole again and finding my inner strength, I had handed it over to Nicholas and let him be the strength. I had thought this would make me feel safe, but in truth it was stifling

me. Soon after moving to Madison, I had decided to open my own home child care business. The old drive to be independent was beginning to resurface. When Rachel was born, my instincts to love her—and be strong for her—kicked it all into high gear. It reminded me of who I once was, that I could be a strong, independent person. I also realized that no matter how tightly I clung to Rachel or how deeply I loved her, she could never replace Joe.

I realized that I had let my fears cloud my vision—my fears of not having a family, a child of my own, someone to love me. I had lost sight of who I was and my goals and ambitions. I had always been a strong independent person. In eighth grade I organized a baseball team. I was editor of my high school yearbook. I saved money and got my first motorcycle and apartment at age eighteen. I co-owned a printing company at twenty. And yet here I was at twenty-seven living the life of a woman who took orders from her husband, had no goals for improvement, and lived each day the same as the last. Nicholas was the perfect husband for that person. But that person was not me. I began to face these issues, and as I did, I began to heal. I found myself again. I found my strength and my confidence. I remembered what made me happy and what didn't. I had spent all these years trying to re-create the picture I had in my head of the perfect little family I had found for Joe and wanted for myself too. But on the Fourth of July, 1991, standing in the kitchen of our home, with a husband, a job, a daughter, and good friends at a barbecue picnic in our backyard, I knew that

I didn't belong there. This was not my life. This had been my dream. But now that I was living it, it felt more like a nightmare.

Nicholas had done exactly what I had wanted someone to do: To be my knight in shining armor and sweep me away to a completely different life. To take away all the burdens that had been weighing so heavily on me for years: responsibility, decisions, financial stability. He took it all away. Then he gave me what I wished for so many times: a husband, a family, a home. At first it felt wonderful, but then it didn't. I felt like an actress playing a part. It was a great show—I was told what to do and say, and I did it. But it wasn't me. I just couldn't pretend to be someone I wasn't any more. When I gave up Joe, I had given away a huge piece of who I was with him. Nicholas took away what was left.

After reconnecting with Lori, I was fortunate enough to attend her wedding. It was so real. Their love was real. The support of family was real. Their shared hopes and dreams were real. I thought of my own wedding, and suddenly I saw it for what it was: a performance—a perfect performance, and not one moment of it was real.

I saw Eric. He had married the girl he had left me for. He described it to me, and again I saw what I had seen at Lori's wedding. It was real people. Real friends. A real love. I could see it in Eric's eyes. I had seen it earlier in Lori's. The love they had for their spouses made them stronger, brought out the best in them. I had thought love was giving yourself to another. I took it too literally. What I was now learning was that love was giving of

yourself—using your strengths to strengthen the other person and being strengthened in return. I had not offered anything to Nicholas because I had nothing of myself to give.

As the years had passed, and the letters from Joe's parents came, I had begun to heal. I felt less needy. Having Rachel need me brought back my remaining strength. I began to assert my independence. I argued with Nicholas more and more. Soon it was every day. Being told what to do by Nicholas now infuriated me. I wanted to make my own decisions—about money, about raising Rachel, about the furniture, about what to cook for supper. The more I tried to be me again, the worse my marriage got. The real me would never have married Nicholas, and I soon realized this.

Ending my marriage brought back all the same hurts that giving up Joe did. I was doing something my church was against, I was disappointing my family, and I was again changing my role in society.

Despite this, I have no regrets about either decision. Getting a divorce was the right thing, not just for me but for my daughter. Having two homes has been a difficult thing in her life, but growing up in a home with no love and growing resentment—even hatred—would have been devastating. She was a strong, independent two-year-old, and she gave me the strength to become a strong and independent role model again so she would never lose her confidence.

After my divorce I swore off men and took up dancing. On the nights when Rachel went to her dad's house,

I would go to a local club that had a big dance floor and played country music. Line dancing had just hit the scene, and I thought it was the best idea ever. I could dance all I wanted to and never needed a partner.

After I'd been dancing alone a couple of months, I met John. He was older and was coming off a divorce, too, and became a sort of substitute for my dad. We could talk for hours about the trials of relationships, and both agreed dancing was much more rewarding than dating. He asked me to join a dance club with him, since his current partner was moving away. When I danced with John, it was like floating on a cloud. I hadn't felt like that since I was two and my dad would waltz me around the living room. I quickly agreed to be John's dance partner.

We submersed ourselves in the dancing, practicing every night for hours. Eventually we traveled together to Knoxville, Tennessee, to tape six shows for Club Dance. It was one of the most exhilarating adventures of my life.

It was also during this time that I met Steve. I was in the club one night when he walked in. I noticed him right away—guys that good-looking didn't typically come into that country bar. I took one look at his amazing eyes and thought, "If I could get a man like that, I'd be swooning like a school girl forever." I waited all night for him to ask me to dance. In the end, the friend he had come with asked me. As I found out much later, they had argued over who would get to ask me and flipped a coin, and Steve had lost. But I had other plans—during our dance I asked his friend to introduce us.

Although there was not a single problem I could find with him when we started to date, I ended it. I just wasn't ready. He was too perfect. I felt as if I might just fall in love, and God knows I didn't want to do that again.

But God had other plans, and he wasn't about to let me screw them up. On my thirtieth birthday my sisters Karen and Jane (who I had long since convinced to move to Madison) took me out to celebrate. We went to a new dance bar, and I ran into this guy I had been seeing for a couple weeks. He told me he had picked up someone else the night before and slept with her. I just turned and walked away. *I'm done*, I thought. *They're all jerks.*

And then, as I was leaving the bar, I ran into Steve. He was so excited to see me again. He told me that he had spent the last six months telling his friends that I was "the one that got away." I laughed. I didn't believe a word of it. He asked the friend he was with (whom I'd never met) to come over and tell me about the one that got away. His friend rolled his eyes and said, "Are you talking about that line-dancer girl again? Give it a rest!" My jaw dropped.

I gave him a second chance. We started dating again, and like before, I instantly felt he could be the guy I would fall in love with. And I did. But worries about Joe stayed on my mind. I told Steve my story, and unlike other guys who then changed the subject, or brushed it off, he hugged me.

I began to settle into my life. I knew marriage was too important to be forced. So I could wait. I knew I would

probably not get to see Joe until he was eighteen. Again, I could wait. Waiting wouldn't mean my life stopped. It just meant that in addition to how good things were at this time, there was a possibility that it would get even better.

Chapter Seven

*B*UILDING *R*ELATIONSHIPS

You know that game that counselors like to make you play, where you stand with your back to someone, close your eyes, and fall backwards, trusting the person will catch you and not let you fall? This is what open adoption can feel like in the beginning, except you have no reason to trust the person who is supposed to catch you because it's a stranger. They haven't done anything to gain your trust, and, likewise, you've done nothing to earn their trust. A birthmother blindly trusts strangers to love her child as their own, to let her know he's happy, and to never deny her existence. Likewise, adoptive parents trust a stranger to give up her child, to make them a family, and to never tear them apart.

Taking this first step of blind trust takes enormous courage, respect, and love. This is the foundation successful open adoptions are built on. But after those first steps are taken, a birthmother releases her child into the care of another, and adoptive parents open a line of communication to reassure the birthmother of her child's happiness. Step by step trust is built, respect grows, and the love that brought everyone into this arrangement blossoms for the benefit of a child.

This chapter will discuss the steps necessary for a successful relationship between adoptive parents and birthmothers. Specifically, they are:

- ♦ Respecting one another.
- ♦ Being honest.
- ♦ Supporting the adoptive parents' role as parents.
- ♦ Facing fears through communication.
- ♦ Growing with the changing relationship.

Whether your arrangement allows for face-to-face meetings, phone calls, ongoing letters, or only annual letters, the steps you take to build a relationship will remain the same. Obviously, the more contact you are able to have, the faster you will build trust and respect. However, slow or fast, it's important that you get there. As you build your relationship over the years, you will find that it changes. You may have difficult times, but the basis you build of respect and honest and open communication will guide you through them. When this process is successful, in the end you will find that the lines between adoptive family and birth family no longer exist—you are just family.

Respecting One Another

In order for any relationship to be successful there needs to be mutual respect. This means understanding that the other person has a point of view—which may be different from your own—and respecting this view. Understanding just how the other person is thinking or feeling about a particular situation can help you to say the things that will make her feel respected. When someone respects your point of view, you are then more likely to be open to her point of view. It's a win-win situation.

I've discussed the point of view of the birthmother a lot so far, and I've also given you some information about the feelings of adoptive parents. Don't believe the myths of the past—look for the truths. Adoptive parents need to understand the truths about birthmothers: First, that they made their choice out of love for their child. Second, that they will most definitely never "forget" their child. Likewise, birthmothers should understand the truths about adoptive parents: First, that they are adopting a child out of love. Second, that they will never forget the birthmother or their gratitude for her gift. What a wonderful place to begin a relationship! Love and gratitude that will never be forgotten. It's a beautiful beginning. Celebrate this.

Being Honest

In the past, secrecy was a big part of adoption. Open adoption is proving that honesty is a much healthier route for everyone involved—most particularly the adoptee. Adoptive parents who had shrouded their life with secrecy in hopes of protecting their new family instead endured years of paranoia. If their child learned the truth at some point, the broken trust often led to the end of their relationship. In addition, since the truth of their birthmothers' motives couldn't be determined because of closed records, the adoptees often felt anger toward their birthmothers as well.

While those within the adoption community have seen the benefits of honesty, the generations before us were so convinced that secrecy was necessary that many in general society hold onto it today. There are people in my family who still believe I should not share my story with anyone, that "letting it out" will do more harm than good. I say with complete certainty that holding it in for years hurt a lot more than talking about it ever could.

Both families, adoptive and birth, are faced with the decision of how honest to be with other family members, friends, and general society. Again, secrecy only leads to pain. It is painful to keep a secret—it automatically comes with feelings of shame. It is also painful when the secret comes out—trust is broken, and often it's difficult or impossible to repair it. Honesty from the start is the best tool for establishing trusting, long lasting relationships.

I often wish I had been able to do this from the beginning. However, I placed my son for adoption during a time when the prevailing social opinion was still very negative about adoption. The usual response when I told my story was one of shock, with comments such as, "I could never give away my child." I believe this is one of the most hurtful statements people can make to a birthmother. The implication is that placing her child for adoption was wrong, that she must not have wanted the child. It's also the reason I have titled this book *Because I Loved You*. Once and for all, I would like everyone to know that placing a child for adoption is not like giving away an old pair of jeans that don't fit. It is being courageous enough to put the child's needs first. It is a very difficult decision based on love.

I no longer hide my story. Photos of my son are all over my house, and anyone who sees them is told directly who he is. No lies. No shame. Just honesty. I learned how to be this forthright from my son. As you'll see in the next chapter, because he was raised with honesty, it came naturally for him. It doesn't even occur to him to lie or feel shame. I can only hope that by sharing our story we've begun to teach the world to do this as well.

Supporting the Adoptive Parents' Role as Parents

With the emergence of open adoption, a new myth began to surface: that being in contact with the birthmother would mean the child now had two mothers. However, as Adam Pertman found in researching his book *Adoption Nation*, "Adoptive and birthparents in ongoing relationships discover another simple but essential truth: Open adoption is not co-parenting." Creating a respectful relationship between birthmothers and adoptive parents means respecting the role of mother. It can be complicated, but it also can be done.

This is the time to remember everyone's motives. Birthmothers who chose open adoption are not looking for a venue to continue being "mother" to their child. What they are most often searching for is a connection that allows them to know their child is well and loved, in order to put their fears to rest. Adoptive mothers have chosen open adoption because they desire to be mothers, but they respect the fact that their child is there because of you.

As you communicate through letters or phone calls or even visits, remember to use language that shows respect. You want your child to have great parents, and in order for parents to be successful, they need to have a close bond with their child—one that is not in danger of being compromised. It can be helpful for both birthmothers and adoptive parents to have some understanding of what the child's developmental needs will be. Here's a general guide:

Infants
Bonding begins immediately at birth. The first few weeks of an infant's life are critical for creating connections with her parents. Physical touch and verbal interaction support brain development in areas of emotional control and social attachment.

Toddlers
Around two years old children begin to seek their independence, yet they are still in need of the security their

parents provide. Creative development begins as they explore the world around them, knowing they have the safety of their parents' arms to return to at any time.

Preschoolers and Kindergarteners

During preschool and kindergarten years children are beginning to understand social relationships more fully. Their own interactions hold increasing importance in their lives. Yet they are still very connected to and need their parents. Because of their increasing social understanding, children's questions about being adopted will most likely take on more detail, and over time they will come to full understanding.

School-age children (six to twelve years)

During these years children are taking all they have learned thus far from their parents into their own world of school and friends and testing this information. Children trust their parents to have been truthful with them. If they discover discrepancies, it can leave them confused and less willing to confide in their parents about personal matters. If an honest, open relationship has been built, children and parents will continue to deepen their relationship. Children will come to their parents for advice and counseling.

Teenagers

These years can present the most difficulties—for adoptive parents and birthmothers alike. Teenagers are trying so hard to find their place in the world. They are exercising every ounce of independence. Sometimes they rebel against parents just for the sake of having a different opinion. This is a time to be very clear with the child that the adoptive parents are still the parents. I will discuss this time period in more detail in the next chapter.

Birthmothers can help their children's development at all ages by doing what they can to reassure adoptive mothers that they respect the adoptive mother as the child's mother.

You can do this by making statements like these:

- "You are John's mother. I would never do anything to jeopardize that relationship."

- "I will support you in any decision you make."

- "John is so lucky to have a mother like you."

- "I will not allow John to use our relationship to be disrespectful to you in any way."

- "You are the mother I had hoped my child would have."

- "I know that parenting decisions are for you to make. I really appreciate it when you ask my opinion, but I respect that the choice is yours."

- "I'm glad John knows he can count on you to be honest with him."

- "It's wonderful to see how close you are."

Saying or writing these statements may come easily for you, or they may be difficult to do. If they are difficult, it will help you to remember that children often are not happy with their parents or disagree with their choices (think of all the times you felt this way as a child!). When this happens, parents can have a difficult time working the issue out with their children. Ultimately, when parents stay firm in their resolve to teach their child to respect their wishes, the child will learn and will grow as a person. However, if the parents' role is undermined in any way, the child will lose respect for the parents and use it as an excuse not to follow their wishes. This creates a major battle that no one wins, especially the child. This occurs in families in which the parents are divorced and one undermines the authority of the other. You do not want this to happen between your child and his parents, and you most certainly don't want to be the reason for it. The more you can support the adoptive mother's authority, the more you will support your child. Model respect for your child; he or she will learn from it.

Facing Fears through Communication

Ongoing communication between adoptive parents and birthmothers allows for fears to be addressed and problems resolved. Adam Pertman writes, "Most reassuring is the fact that there's no clinical or practical evidence to indicate adoptees or birthparents try to disrupt or interfere with adoptions that include sustained contact. To the contrary, many adoptions grow stronger and all three members of the triad become more secure when their relationships cease to be based on fear and fantasy."

When everyone feels secure and respected, it is easier to go deeper and address any fears as they arise. As always, it's important to take the time to think about the

181

other point of view. Put yourself in their shoes. Think of what fears you would have. Then do all you can to calm those fears for that person.

As your respect for and understanding of the other person grows, so will your love. You will care enough about them to not want them to be scared or worried. You will want to help them to feel safe, secure, and happy. When you take the first step in voicing a potential fear, the gratitude the other person feels will be evident, and it will create a stronger bond between you.

I often worried for my son's mother. During the first few years after I placed Joe with her, there were many awful stories in the news about birthmothers who tried to take back their children. I understood how scary the thought would be for her, and I cared enough about her not to want to see her scared. I took the initiative to write about these cases when they occurred and to reassure her it would never happen with us. The idea of breaking the loving bond I had set up to develop between my son and her seemed cruel—both to her and to my son. I would never even consider it. Her relief in the return letters was evident. With each exchange our concern for each other grew, and our bond tightened.

Growing with the Changing Relationship

As time passes and open, honest communication continues, trust grows. The more trust each side has for the other, the more comfortable each feels in opening up further or in having more contact. This may occur quickly or over a period of years. The frequency of communications affects the length of time it will take to build trust.

If the original adoption arrangement was semi-open, as trust grows, there is usually a tendency to increase the openness of the arrangement. This is a positive development for everyone involved, as face-to-face contact will allow everyone to bond on a deeper level. It is especially beneficial to the adoptee. Most adoptees, but not all, have a need to understand their personal history. As with any subject, understanding the past can be key to determining the future. It does not dismiss the present.

My son wanted to ask questions such as: Where did I get this dark hair? Why do I have this musical talent? Why am I so tall? In essence, what he wanted to know was, am I the only one like me? Or do I have a connection with others who have these traits too?

The biggest question looming for a birthmother is the day her child looks into her eyes and asks, "Why did you give me up?" Such a brief question, but with an enormous impact. It seems as though it requires a simple answer, yet choosing adoption for one's child is anything but simple. It takes courage, intelligence, selflessness, and love. The reasons are numerous and often complicated. Giving a child the answer he or she is seeking is often a frightening moment for a birthmother.

Whether the openness of the adoption allows the birthmother to see her child through his young years, or not until he is older, the time comes when the child is old enough to ask this question and expect real answers. The timing for this meeting is a very personal decision for all those involved. The key to its success is honesty. Sharing honestly any fears and respecting the fears of the other parties will lay a foundation of understanding that over-comes the obstacles.

It all comes back to trust. Adoptive parents need to trust that their role as parents will not be threatened. Birthmothers need to trust that they will be able to build a new relationship with their child, one that is beneficial to each of them. It can be very scary for all those involved, but the rewards can be overwhelming.

Meeting face-to-face is a powerful event. There is a flood of emotions that come along with the flood of questions everyone has. But if a respectful relationship has been built over the years between the adoptive family and the birthmother and the child has been a part of this cir-cle of respect, the details in the answer to that heavy question "Why?" will lose their importance. It will be clear to everyone involved, including the child, that there is only one answer: "Because I loved you."

Open adoption is no longer a destination without a plan. It's found a happy ending and those entering into this arrangement today have stories such as mine to guide them on their journey. While it still requires the courage to fall back on strangers and trust them to catch you, knowing the potential for love and respect will give you the strength to go ahead and fall.

BECAUSE *I* MISSED YOU

In 1992, the now infamous "Baby Jessica" case exploded on the news circuit. A birthfather claimed his parental right to a child who had been placed for adoption. He was awarded custody, and at two years old the child was taken from the adoptive parents and returned. As Joe's seventh birthday approached and I waited for my annual letter, I realized how scared Jerry and Kathy, his parents, must have been that first year of his life, and that they might still be scared. I had no doubts about their love for him, and I was so thankful that he had them in his life that I wanted nothing but happiness for them as a family. I wrote to them first that year, telling them that I had no regrets, that I knew how deeply they loved him, and how thankful I was that they could give him all I could not. I talked about the "Baby Jessica" case and did all I could to ease any fears they might have. My wish for them was a home absent of fear and filled with love. In their return letter it was obvious that I had guessed correctly, and that they needed to hear all I had said. Our respect for each other grew tremendously that year and continued to with each year as we placed our fears on the table and shared what was in our hearts.

Joe's parents, like any adoptive parents, had fears of losing him but had decided from the start that honesty would be a stronger weapon against this fear than secrecy. They placed a picture of me in Joe's room and answered his questions about who I was in an open, caring, and honest way. They followed his lead, providing only what he asked for and waiting for him to ask the questions before providing the answers. At two, Joe asked, "Who's that?" They answered, "Your birthmother." At five he asked, "Was I in your tummy, Mommy?" They answered, "No, you were in Pat's tummy, but now you are with Mommy." Because they always gave him the answers he sought, his trust in them was unquestioned. Because he was assured of my love for him as well, it too was never questioned.

I couldn't have been more relieved. I had a friend who was eighteen when she found out she was adopted. It was devastating for her. The fact that she was an adopted child wasn't what hurt—it was the realization that for eighteen years her parents had been lying to her. It broke the trust in their relationship so deeply that two years passed before she would even speak to them again. It was heartbreaking to consider that this could happen to my child. Just as they had to put their trust in me, I had to put my trust in Jerry and Kathy. All I could do was try to dispel their fears of me, to let them know I would not try to harm their position as Joseph's parents, and to stress that I would not return to tear him away from them.

It meant forcing myself to back away and let go of every decision for Joseph. I couldn't tell them what to do or even suggest what I would like them to do as parents. This was such a difficult task that from the beginning I wrote them long letters assuring them of my role, telling them I thought of myself as Joe's guardian angel, not a parent—someone who would pray for him everyday, think of him always, but physically not be in his life. I didn't realize until much later that I was writing these letters as much to convince myself as I was to convince them.

It turned out that what helped me to finally let go, a little more each year, was not the letter I wrote to them but the letter they wrote to me. With each letter I read, it became clearer that these were loving, supportive, thoughtful parents. I also saw that they were providing him with the life that I could not have. It became almost impossible to question whether or not I had made the right choice—it was so obvious that I had. A year after the "Baby Jessica" case, I quit writing the letters assuring them I would not change my mind. There was no need to. It was now a fact.

As time passed we each experienced all the fears that have led many birthmothers and adoptive parents to believe myths about adoption. For me, it was wondering if they thought I placed Joe for adoption because I didn't care, or if they thought I could or should forget him. For them, it was wondering if secrecy would have been better or if Joe would resent them if he couldn't know me.

However, we all faced our fears head on. We wrote to each other and talked about our fears, and each time, as a letter was returned full of love, respect, and understanding, the fear was put to rest. We built a relationship built on the truths. The truth that we all loved Joe dearly. The truth that we all wanted him to have every opportunity to grow and develop into an amazing adult. The truth that life was moving forward for us all, with new challenges, new joys, and new accomplishments. As our lives changed, so did our relationship.

When Joe was born, and I chose Kathy and Jerry to be his parents, we started with just one step. We all blindly trusted a stranger not to break our hearts and had faith that this arrangement could become a blessing for this child. None of us had control of the things that we feared in this partnership, but we all soon realized that we did have the power to take that fateful first step of trust and the second step of honest communication. The fact that we all took those steps is what set us all free of our fears.

We were able to build a relationship, establish boundaries we were comfortable with, and move forward in our lives. But as Joe grew older, the boundaries we had established in the beginning fell away, and a whole new beginning faced us.

In 1997, I had been divorced from Nicholas for four years. My sisters Karen and Jane were both living in Madison now; Jane and I were sharing a house. My home child care business was flourishing. Rachel was seven years old. Steve and I had been dating for three years. It

was naptime at my day care, and time to execute the ritual I did at this time every year. I opened the front door, ignoring the peeling paint. Stepped down the front stoop, putting aside a tricycle left behind. Walked down the short sidewalk, stopping to smell the fragrance of my beloved yellow roses (the only flower I seem able to grow). Walked down the driveway, admiring the fading drawings of rainbows the children had made earlier in the week. Stepped into the road and faced the mailbox.

I placed my hand on the door, said my simple prayer, "Dear God, please let it be there," and opened the door. Longingly peering inside I spotted a flyer from another preschool curriculum company. I held my breath as I picked it up. My heart racing, I reached in again, picking up a bill for my student loan, then caught my breath as I saw the familiar envelope with the blue Catholic Charities logo in the corner. I stood still staring at it a moment. Then I grabbed the envelope, shoved the rest of the mail I had taken out back into the mailbox, slammed the door, and ran into the house.

I held the envelope in my hands, smoothing it onto my lap, feeling its thickness. I felt a pang of disappointment as I realized it was not hard and stiff—indicating there would be no photos. My eyes started to tear as I turned it over and loosened the flap. I pulled the one page letter out, again feeling disappointment because it was so short. Then I read: "We would like to arrange a visit with you and your family in the near future, possibly a day for picnicking and visiting in Dubuque or some other mutual location at your suggestion."

My heart stopped. I couldn't breathe. I read it again. And again. Then everything switched gears—my heart raced, I was panting, my entire body tingled and ached, and I started to cry. Not only did they want to meet, but they wrote about it so casually, as though it were a common occurrence to get together. Once again I was struck by how kind and open his parents were. There had never been an awkward word in any of their letters.

On the other hand, I was hysterical. I clutched the letter and ran for the phone to call my mother at work. She answered, and I screamed into the phone, "E aunts oo mee mee!" Then I sobbed and screamed some more.

Mom stayed calm. "Dear, calm down. I can't understand you. Are you all right?"

I took a deep breath and cried again, "He wants to meet me!"

"Who?" she asked.

"Joe! His parents! All of them!" I started to ramble. "I got their letter today, and Jerry said they want to meet with me and you and everyone, and in Dubuque I think, and he asked it all calm like it was no big deal and he wrote all about Joe and how he likes fishing but that he doesn't like biking as much as they do, but they want to come and they want to see us, all of us. . . ."

Mom interrupted me. "Calm down, Patty. This is great news! Did they say when?" She was crying, too, now.

"No, I'm supposed to write back I think, or call Catholic Charities. I'm not sure!" My crying subdued to an occasional sob now.

"Oh baby, I'm so happy for you," Mom said. "Why don't you write a letter to them and to Nancy? We could meet at the campground or somewhere in Dubuque."

"I'll do it right now," I answered.

We made the arrangements through Nancy at Catholic Charities. She was very excited about it and assured me everything would work out great. I had a million questions and concerns, and she suggested I write about them to Jerry and Kathy. My main concern centered on the fact that Joe was only twelve years old. I knew I would be in a highly emotional state because I had played the scene a million times over the years. Only, in my mind, the part of Joe was played by a young man who was strong and could handle the hugging and tears of a blubbering birthmother. The real Joe was not a man yet. He was a boy. I was afraid of scaring him to the point of withdrawal and losing the chance of ever getting close to him. I also wanted to know what his expectations were, if any. Why now? For what purpose?

Meeting Joseph's needs was anything but a new concept for me, and as always I wanted to do what was best for him. I also had concerns about Jerry and Kathy. I respected them as Joe's parents and wanted to be sure this was their wish as well. I wanted to assure them I would always feel this way and would not allow Joe to disrespect them as a result of meeting me. As in the beginning, I hoped for this to be right for everyone involved. I wanted them to know I would do all I could to be sure it was.

After writing these concerns and some general questions about the details, I also wrote my second letter ever directly to my son. As easily and quickly as my thoughts filled the pages of the letter I wrote to Jerry and Kathy, the one to Joseph was impossible to begin. I stared at the blank sheet before me, my mind racing with thoughts, all fighting to emerge first. My mind dove into its storage of language, searching for the perfect words—each word, each syllable, each thought had to be perfect. No mistakes, no confusion. It felt like waiting outside a closed door for twelve years and finally it had opened—just a crack. A sliver of light was pouring through, and I knew that if the right words were chosen it could open the door and the light from within would spill forth, enveloping me and filling my life. But if the words were wrong, the key would be lost, and the light would go out as the door shut forever. Putting words on paper has always been a task of ease and comfort for me. But now I felt tense, scared, apprehensive to put even his name in ink. After a half hour passed unnoticed, I decided to trust the pen and dive into the words. I wrote slowly but steadily and tried in those two short pages to convey twelve years' worth of love, concern, pride, and anticipation in a manner that would ease his mind and calm his soul.

I realized after finally putting a stamp to it and releasing it to the postman that it was an undue amount of pressure to put on such a small note. But I said a short prayer nonetheless, hoping it met all his needs for the moment and asking for the strength to meet those needs in the future.

Although it didn't answer all of my questions, the letter I received in reply assured me that we were doing the right thing for Joseph. I was especially touched by the insight I was given into Joseph's feelings. He apparently didn't voice his thoughts on being adopted too often, but Jerry wrote to share with me one of the moments when Joe opened up. Jerry said that they had read my letters with Joe, including the first one I wrote to Joseph the day he was born. I tried desperately in that letter to let him know how I felt about him and why I made the decision I did. To this day I honestly don't remember what I wrote; it's amazing to me that I even actually did it. What I do remember is how much love I felt and how I tried to send a lifetime of love in one small letter for him to have in case I never had the chance to give it in person.

Jerry said that later that evening Joe had asked him, "Do you think she said 'I love you' so many times because she's afraid I'll be mad she gave me up?" Then he continued, in a matter-of-fact tone, "I'm not mad, and I love her very much." I will be forever amazed at Joe's perception and honesty—of all the questions I might have had, he seemed to know which one was the one I needed to be answered the most.

Reading those words in Jerry's letter made my heart jump. I felt the clouds that had accumulated slowly over twelve years begin to dissipate and rise. The cork I had placed in my heart was pushed out, and all my love, fear, happiness, and sadness spilled forth as I collapsed on the couch, tears falling, hands shaking, wailing my thanks to God for all he had done.

Because I Loved You

The details were arranged, and in June 1997 I would finally see my son again. The day came quickly. I changed clothes four times. Paced. Changed again. I had thought it would be a hot day, and it turned out to be chilly. I had waited too long for this moment not to be perfect—right down to my outfit. I wanted him to be proud of how I looked. I wanted his approval of everything about me. I started to doubt that this was a good idea. Maybe he wouldn't like me. Maybe he would just realize how lucky he was not to have me for his mother and go home and never think of me again. I didn't think I could bear to say good-bye twice.

But I couldn't pass up the chance to hold him just once more. To say "I love you" to his face one more time. It would be worth reliving the pain.

Two hours before we were due to meet them at Eagle Point Park in Dubuque, I wanted to leave. Mom, bless her, was steady as a rock, light-hearted, and very amused by my tension. She agreed to leave early, and off we went. It was a beautiful sunny day, big white fluff-balls hanging in the sky, and a cool breeze moving the warm summer air.

The drive seemed to take hours, even days, until we turned onto the small road going into the park. Suddenly I felt as though all time had vanished—the drive there and the twelve years it took to get there seemed like moments, and the fear of not being ready seized my entire body.

We pulled around the bend, and the road opened to a circle, the grand statue of a bald eagle about to take

flight marking the center, as if to guard it for me and this moment. I knew the green van was theirs. I knew within it was the family I couldn't be. We pulled up behind it, and I watched the doors open as I held my breath.

Jerry was first. As I got out of our car and walked toward him, I felt a sudden calmness. Nervousness is for meeting strangers, and this was no stranger. I knew his smile, I knew his eyes, I knew his heart. This was the loving father my child deserved. This man gave me peace of mind and could never make me scared. I instantly knew a closeness that is usually associated with people you see everyday in your life. I felt as though I already knew what it was like to watch his face change as he spoke or to feel the warmth and security of his hugs. Without thought of proper protocol for meeting someone for the first time, I ran to his arms and hugged him as I would my own father. He held me as we both cried, and I knew that he had loved my Joe, that his hugs were there when mine could not be, and like all the best fathers just his presence would make you feel that everything would be all right.

As I let go of Jerry, I looked over and saw Kathy. Tears already forming in her eyes, she stood still, apprehension filling the space between us. Simultaneously we broke the silence and space and hugged. Through the tears I tried to whisper the years of gratitude, but the "thank you" seemed so small in comparison to her years of selfless, devoted love. Then I realized she was thanking me also. With one look we became one person. Together, we were Joe's mother. And instead of any sense of

jealousy over the other's part in that role, we each knew a sense of completion and thankfulness.

I wiped my tears and smiled at her. She was perfect. They were perfect. God had listened, I thought. I spent months praying for the perfect parents for my son, and either there is a God or I have amazing magical powers. Here they are. They are all I wished for and more. "Thankful" doesn't come close to describing the gratitude, amazement, and love I felt toward these two human beings.

And then there was Joe. The next few moments I don't recall. I think we may have said "Hello," maybe not. It doesn't really matter. Life went on fast forward, and I reached out to hug him. Then he was in my arms, and someone abruptly hit "pause." I held him close, my chin resting on the top of his head, the hair fuzzy from his fresh buzz cut. I squeezed him so hard I felt him catch his breath, and when I said, "I'm sorry," he said, "It's okay," and let me hold him still. I felt the weight of my words and his and how they conveyed so much more than that moment.

I knew him, my heart knew him, and now my senses knew him. I pulled back and looked into his eyes, a reflection of my own. Deep, dark pools filled to the brim with wonder, curiosity, and excitement. The eyebrows I remembered. I had spent an entire afternoon memorizing them. The ears too. The soft brown color of his skin, the dimple by his mouth, the way he stood, it was all a collage of me, my father, and my cousins the Polfer boys. He could pass for their brother, I thought.

Then I realized I was still holding him. I laughed and said, "I know I should let go now—I don't want to scare you away." Again the little angel answered, "It's okay." The tears were still falling, and it finally hit me that Joe was a child meeting a stranger who seemed unable to function without crying. This was not the first impression I wanted to make. I knew him, but he did not know me.

Upon seeing Joe, I had once again become the young girl from twelve years ago. But it was time now to be the grown up I had become and move past what I was feeling to focus on what he was feeling and what he needed from me. Twelve years ago it was about me and my loss when he was gone. But he was here now, and it was his time, not mine.

I let him go, and my mother stepped up to us. I introduced her, and she hugged him too. I couldn't believe how natural the scene felt. She looked at him as though she had seen him every day for years and this was just another warm hug from Grandma—not the first one. My mom's ease made me jealous, I admit.

An hour later, we decided to go to a restaurant together for lunch. Throughout dinner I found it hard not to stare. I was absolutely amazed at the familiarity of his actions and motions. His face lit up the same way that Rachel's did when she got excited about something. He talked about the same things I was interested in at his age. He loved music, as did everyone in my family. He loved the outdoors, again as everyone in my family did. We seemed to appreciate the same things, be bothered by the same things, and get excited about the same things.

His body language was so close to Rachel's that I had to blink and shake my head to remember it was him and not her sitting next to me.

We agreed they would come out to my parents' house and campground the following day, and they would get to meet the rest of the family. We also decided to invite Nancy Kinley. We said good-bye in the parking lot—amid many a hug, but the tears were no longer there, only smiles.

Dad and Rachel were waiting for us back at my parents' house. We spent the evening sharing every detail we could remember, and everyone went to sleep that night with great anticipation. Rachel was so excited to finally meet her big brother. She had always known about Joe. She had a photo of him in her room, and we talked about him often. She was six years old at the time of our reunion and had really just started to understand all of it the year before. Since I got divorced, it had been just Rachel and me, and we both loved the idea that there was more to our family. She was a little scared—she really wanted him to like her. I almost laughed as she said it and assured her that they were so much alike it would be impossible for them not to like each other. Joe had said he was excited to meet her as well, and since he was the youngest of his parents' three adopted children, it was a very cool idea to him to be a BIG brother and not the baby of the family.

When Kathy, Jerry, and Joe arrived the next morning, Mom and I greeted them, then introduced them to Rachel, my dad, my sisters, Karen, Jane, and Sue, my grandmother, my aunt Mary Jane Polfer, and Nancy. Everyone commented about how much Joe resembled my Aunt Mary Jane's four boys. They had always looked amazingly similar, each possessing the unmistakable look of a Flogel (my maternal grandparents). Joe didn't see the resemblance, but Grandma put an end to it all when she held Joe's face and kissed his forehead, saying, "There's my Flogel baby."

As the morning progressed, everyone quickly became comfortable together. There was no denying that Joe was one of us. My dad got out his dulcimer, and Joe picked up my mom's guitar, and soon we were all gathered around the kitchen singing together. As Joe's dad and I stood side by side, he put his arm around me and gave me a squeeze. "I just can't get over it," he said. "Watching your dad is like seeing an older version of Joe—they couldn't be more alike."

"I feel the same way," I answered. "For me it's like seeing a younger version of Dad. No wonder they clicked so easily."

Jerry looked into my eyes and said, "It's so obvious Joe is a part of this family, and that makes all of you a part of our family. This just all feels so right. How great is this for Joe, to have this connection with his grandfather. We're going to be coming here a lot more often." We stood together and watched as a young boy and his grandfather deepened their bond over a chorus of "Hymn to Joy."

Later that day I took Joe out for a ride on the Mississippi on my waverunner. We veered off into a backwater stream, pulling up to stop on a wide sandbar. We sat quietly for a while, side by side. And then I said, "I thought you would like to have some time where we could talk." He didn't say anything, so I kept going. "Is there anything you have questions about? I'll answer anything you want to know."

Joe looked down at the water for a moment. Then he looked up at me with those deep brown eyes, the same eyes everyone in my family has, shrugged softly, and said, "Not really, I just missed you. That's all."

I cried as I leaned down to kiss the top of his head and hug him. "I missed you too," I whispered.

We sat another moment or two; then I decided to be sure he wasn't just too scared to ask. "Why did you want to meet me now?"

"I just wanted to get to know you better," he said. He looked so innocent. It was obvious he had no hidden agenda. The questions I thought I would face were the questions of an adult, not a twelve-year-old. Joe was just a boy who wanted to get to know the person he had been told was his first mother. And that's all.

Joe seemed to sense my shock at not being grilled further, and he added, "I told my dad that I could tell by your letters you loved me."

It was getting harder to hold back the tears. "I most certainly do, Joseph, with all my heart."

"Well, I just figured that I ought to get to know someone that can love me that much. So I asked if we could come see you."

"I'm certainly glad you did," I answered. "Everyone has missed you so much, and Rachel is very excited to finally meet her big brother."

"She's cool," he said.

I laughed. When we pulled into the boat landing, Rachel was waiting for us. I let Joe take off to play with her at the campground, and I spent some time talking with Nancy.

We stood on the deck and watched Joe giving Rachel a piggyback ride below us in the campground, running around the apple trees. Nancy took my hand and said, "This is the way it's supposed to be."

I squeezed her hand. "It's pretty amazing isn't it? Look at them. They look so right together." I started crying again.

Nancy sighed. "I wish I could bring people here to see this. I've been telling people for years that if everyone would just trust each other that this is what it could be like, but no one believes it. Everyone still believes this is wrong, that in the end it will hurt someone. How can anyone look at this scene and see something bad?"

"I have no idea," I answered. "You were the one that made this happen. We wouldn't be together today without you." I turned and looked straight at her. "Thank you." We hugged and cried a little more, then stood and watched as Rachel fell completely in love with her big brother.

As the end of the afternoon came, I started to feel heaviness in my throat. I wasn't sure how I could ever say good-bye to Joe again. It just brought back too much sadness, and I knew that this was a happy time—with a

promising future. There was no room for sadness in this farewell.

When the time did come to part ways, we posed for pictures, and there were dozens of hugs all around. I took Joe into my arms and held him tight. I kissed the top of his head, then leaned in, and whispered into his ear, "I promise I'll never say good-bye to you again." We hugged a moment more. When he pulled away, he looked up, smiled, and said "See you later!"

I smiled through the tears as I watched him go, because I knew it was true.

Chapter Eight

NO ROOM FOR REGRET

Even with the ongoing communication supported by open adoption, until the child becomes an adult, it feels as though everyone involved is part of an ongoing story. When all is said and done, and the child becomes independent of mothers and fathers with a life of his or her own, will everyone come together to celebrate the success of adoption, or will there be regrets?

The adolescent years bring many changes, for both child and parents. By relying on the base of respect and trust that has been built over the years, everyone will be able to evolve in their relationships as well. This chapter will cover that bumpy road called "the teenage years" and help guide you toward finding your own happy endings. We'll discuss the following topics:

- ♦ Changing relationships.
- ♦ Surviving adolescence together.
- ♦ Celebrating the experience.

You've made it this far, and while the teen years may feel like they last longer than the previous twelve years did, they will be over soon! In the end, there will be an adult whose most prominent characteristics are a capacity for love, respect, and understanding because he was surrounded by it his entire life.

Changes in Relationships

This will most likely be a time to redefine the birthmother's role. Identifying what role a birthmother plays in her child's life and subsequently what role the child plays in the birthmother's life can be very confusing. "The reflected message from society about the role of an adopted child to a birthmother simply parallels the birthmother's own conundrum: no role, a nominal role (adopted child) that is ignored socially, or an ambiguous role (my oldest child but not the oldest child I am parenting; a child for whom I am a parent, but not *the* parent)" (Fravel, McRoy, and Grotevant). These identity issues exist regardless of the level of openness and therefore must be addressed.

I faced this dilemma. However, I knew that although I was not Joe's mother, and I wasn't even sure exactly what our relationship was, I wanted to find out. Whether you have direct contact with your child or contact only through letters or phone calls, it is during the teenage years that your child will most likely want to connect with you more. It will be important to continue to support the adoptive parents' authority as parents. But it is possible to do this as well as establish a new role for yourself in your child's life.

When Joe lost those illusions about my becoming his mother again, he soon realized that he just wanted to get to know me. He wanted to know why he's so musical, why his eyes are so dark, why he prefers riding a motorcycle. I knew why—because of me. As we muddled through establishing a new relationship, we were amazed at the similarities we found. Apparently this is not something new. As Merry Bloch Jones writes, "Similarities in careers, personalities and predicaments were discovered again and again by birthmothers who met their relinquished children later in life, as adults."

I may not be Joe's mother anymore, and as a young man he didn't need me to be, but I am Joe's family. I am his past, and he is my future. When I am gone, he will be a piece of me left on this earth; I am proud and honored to see the effect he has on this world. Finding a way to label this relationship may be impossible. Or you may have an idea of one that suits you. I have heard many over the years: "other mother," "first mother," or simply "birthmother." In the end, I felt any title with the word "mother" in it somehow took away from his adoptive mother. I felt that Kathy was the one who deserved the title "mother." So we settled for "Pat." Nice and simple. While this dilemma of labels did cause us confusion for awhile, in the end we realized that the labels didn't matter. What mattered was that we knew we loved each other, that we were family, that we would always be connected in a special way, and that we were on our way to being good friends. It didn't matter that we couldn't sum it up in one word.

Surviving Adolescence —Together

As I write this, Rachel is now entering high school. I am in no way prepared to say that I can lead you through teenage years without any bumps—I know all too well just how complicated this time is! However, I do believe that there are some general guidelines that can help ease some of the fears and handle some of the challenges for both birthmothers and adoptive parents. Let's first take some time to understand the developmental needs of a teenager; then we can explore how knowing these aspects can help us avoid any potential pitfalls.

Developmental needs of teenagers
(ages twelve to eighteen)

Children at this age go through something very similar to what they did as young toddlers—a desire to be independent conflicting with a desire to be close to family. Teenagers need parents to support this independence. If they feel their parents trust them, they will trust themselves.

During times of conflict with parental authority, it is common for teenagers (whether or not they are adopted) to fantasize about being in a different family—a fantasy family in which there are no rules. Teenagers challenge parental authority as a way to assert their own independence—not specifically to hurt parents. Clear boundaries are necessary in order to avoid power battles.

Teenagers are trying to discover their own identity during this time. They will question everything about themselves in order to come to an understanding of who they are. Part of this puzzle is understanding their biol-ogy—what is the way it is because of family genetics and what is unique to them.

How your child navigates these milestones is hard to predict. Each child is an individual and has her own set of needs, fears, and successes. I sincerely hope your child's successes far outnumber any conflicts arising from needs and fears. When I remember back to those years in my life, I am stunned that my parents ever made it through alive with four teenage girls in the house! This is not an easy time. Don't feel that you have failed simply because some weeks get tough—give yourself a break.

If birthmothers respect the fact that adoptive parents are going to deal with parenting a teenager on a daily ba-sis, and concede the difficulty of this task, it will go a long way toward everyone working together.

Joe had his own share of difficult times during ado-lescence. However, his mother and I discussed our fears and supported each other's positions. I saw quickly that it was important for me to distance myself from Joe slightly during those years. It was an extremely difficult task, as we had only recently started to visit each other. But I had a profound respect for the years of love that his mother had shown him, and I refused to be a part of any games he would play that would hurt her.

On one occasion, Joe did what I'm sure any young man would do: he took a look at my life and imagined himself still being a part of it, imagined that I had kept him. While this may be a nice fantasy for a child, as adults we know better. My sister quickly pulled Joe back to reality by pointing out how all of our lives would have proceeded much differently had we kept him. What he saw now would not even exist. It was futile to imagine being a part of it. My choice affected every aspect of my future and that of my family, as I'm sure it does for all birthmothers.

Looking back, it is easy to see this. Nicholas would never have dated someone with a child—which meant I never would have moved to Wisconsin, which meant I never would have talked my two sisters into moving there as well, which meant Karen never would have met her husband, and so on, and so on. My family, my career, where I lived would have all been different.

Remember that it is normal for a teenager to fantasize about a different life. Many who are not adopted actually fantasize that they are adopted just as an outlet to imagine a different family. These thoughts do not mean that the child doesn't love her family, or even that she truly wishes she lived a different life. It is just an emotional outlet for any restrictions of her independence she may be feeling. Think of it as equivalent to punching a pillow when you get mad. It's never because you hate pillows! The best way to deal with any fantasy of a child is to present him with realities. Since he is getting closer to adulthood, he does have the skills to identify and process reality when it is presented to him. Take the time to address the issue; don't wait for it to go away. Your child needs someone to pull him out of the fantasy and get his life back on track.

This is not an issue that needs to turn into a conflict or power play. Demanding that a child respect where they live and the family they have never works. You've shown him his whole life that respect is earned and appreciated, not forced. So don't change the game now. Birthmothers may need to pull back on their level of involvement for a while in order for the child to get back on track. Or a heartfelt long talk about the issue may be all that is needed. This is an important time for birthmothers and adoptive parents to communicate.

This is not a time to let the fears seep back into the relationship. Communication is important at this venture. Adoptive parents and birthmothers need to share their thoughts and fears and work together. Communication will be important to the child as well: they will need to share their feelings with their adoptive parents, and they may feel a need to ask questions of their birthmother. Hopefully, trust has been built over the years that will make this possible. The communication that occurs from the beginning builds and grows and creates a solid relationship over time that can endure the trials of the teenage years.

Celebrate the Experience

When you've made it through those last years of childhood, take the time to reconnect with each other and celebrate the life of this child everyone loves. Take time to express your gratitude, your love. Be proud of all the tough choices that had to be made and the tough years you made it through.

You may have had meetings with your child and his family for years; you may have only been doing it a short time; you may be hoping it will happen soon. Whatever your arrangement, if you have been successful in building trust and respect over the years, you will most likely choose to get together when your child becomes an adult. I sincerely hope that you take this chance. There is something about getting together to celebrate each other and all you've been through. Many might refer to it as "closure," but you will find that rather than feeling that a door is closing, you feel as though it has finally been completely opened!

When you spend eighteen years being completely open and honest with another person, building trust, earning respect, gaining respect, creating understanding, what you will have is a relationship that will last beyond specific dates. You will forever be connected. You will forever care about each other. You will be family.

OUR GRADUATION

The reunion with Joe, and meeting his parents for the first time, became a turning point in my life. The fears I had clung to were gone, the worries evaporated into the sky. I had made it through. Joe had made it through. And we were both going to be all right.

I was ready to move on, to trust in love again. Just two months later, Steve proposed on the top of the cliff looking over my parents' campground. It was the hottest day of the summer, and he had made both our parents and his godparents take the hike up the hill with us so they would all be there. I cried so hard I couldn't open my eyes, but just as when Joe was born, my mom was there to say, "Open your eyes and answer him!" After jumping into his arms with a resounding "Yes!" I went to the cliff's edge and screamed, "He finally asked me to marry him!" Someone from the campground below yelled up, "What did you say?" And I screamed "Yes!" as we all laughed and cried together.

We were married on a hilltop as well, in a tiny chapel Steve's ancestors had helped to build, with the same people by our side. Just before the ceremony he handed me yellow roses and a card. It said, "I'm glad I met you."

The reception was in that campground, the place where all the best things in my life had happened. And Joe was there. So were his parents. We were all one family now, and having them there to share the day meant everything to me. Joe even got out his guitar and sang a song with the band for me. My dad played the washboard. And it was wonderful.

It was real. Real friends. Family—all of my family. A real love. I had finally found what Lori and Eric had found in their marriages—a love that made me stronger, better. While waiting for my brother-in-law to arrive with my dress, I had a moment of panic as I thought the event was not going to proceed as planned. Without realizing, I had slipped into the role of bride once more, as I had when I married Nicholas. And once again, my mom was there to pull me out of the fog. She grabbed me by the shoulders and yelled, "Who's your best friend?"

I thought, *Why is she asking me a ridiculous question like that right now? My dress is not here!* I hadn't answered her, so she said it again, "Who is your best friend?"

"Steve," I answered without thinking.

Mom smiled. "You are going to spend the rest of your life with your best friend, who loves you dearly and whom you love. Isn't that all that matters today?" She was right. I immediately calmed down, and from that moment forward the only thing that mattered was the love I felt around me that entire day.

As Joe grew into his teenage years, not only did his body go through drastic changes, but his relationship with his parents, and with me, had growing pains. He went from short and a bit pudgy with a shaved head to a tall, thin, dark-haired hunk. His attitude grew right along with his height, and he starting searching for his independence.

As all teenagers do, he tested his parents, and he had fantasies about a different life with me. When he was fourteen, he came to stay with my parents for a week. That weekend Steve and I and Karen and her husband camped in their campground and spent time with Joe. We had brought our waverunners and had a blast all weekend out on the river. Sunday afternoon Karen and Joe had gone up to Mom's house to get some supplies, and Joe said to her, "I can't believe I missed all this."

Karen asked what he meant. He said that we seemed to have such great lives and he wished he could have been a part of all of it. Karen understood that he was thinking that if I had kept him, the fun he had just experienced that weekend would be his everyday life. She quickly set him straight.

Karen told Joe firmly that everything he saw around him that day would not exist if I had kept him. She explained how each member of my family was affected by that decision and how it set our lives in courses that were different from what they would have been otherwise. She pointed out that she knew that if I had kept Joe I would have stayed in Dubuque. This meant Karen would have never taken the chance to move to Madison. She

never would have met her husband or switched careers and been as successful as she was. The waverunners, our cars, our lifestyles, our husbands all would have been different. She told him he was foolish to believe that this is what his life would have been. She told him to be thankful for all he did have because if I had kept him, he most likely would not have had half of the opportunities his parents had given him. My family had too much respect for his parents to allow him to be disrespectful in any way.

When she told me about the conversation, I decided to back away for awhile. Since meeting, Joe and I had begun writing to each other. He was visiting my parents a couple times a year, and I would always join him there. But for the remainder of his teen years I only sent short cards, and I only stayed for a day if he was at my parents. A few times I didn't go at all. It was very painful to do this, but I'm glad I did. My family had a very difficult time understanding. It was so easy for them to be his family—it didn't infringe on anyone's feelings. But I knew that by getting close to him during these years I was risking having him fantasizing even more about having me for a mother instead of Kathy. That was something I absolutely couldn't tolerate. I wasn't about to let him believe for a second that if she made him mad (which every mother of a teenager will do eventually!) that he could decide to run away from her and come to me. Again, I knew I had to let go in order for him to grow.

I called his mother a year later, and we had a long discussion about how tough the teenage years were. I

told her why I felt I needed to pull back and that I hoped he would understand some day. I knew it confused him when I did. I shared with her my story, which I had never done before, of how I came to be pregnant and how I reached the decision I did. I wanted her to understand how strongly I felt about her being Joe's mother. I had made that choice for him years ago, and I wasn't about to take it away from her now.

She wrote me a letter afterwards. It was so beautiful that I would like to share it with you now:

> *Dear Pat,*
>
> *I've been wanting to write since our Saturday phone conversation and tell you how much that meant to me. The older I get the more I realize that being young can be the hardest time in our lives. Certainly we have all this potential that we'll never have any other time in our lives, but it is certainly hard to deal with all the set backs and you certainly had them piled on you all in that one year. It took me years to learn that the rest of our life is whatever we want it to be regardless of what happens today. Knowing you and reading your letters over the last 15 years I know you learned that lesson early and well and you certainly have gone on to achieve many wonderful things. I hope that your successes have diminished the pain but that also the difficulties of that year have made you appreciate what you have been given now.*
>
> *I know this is the case with me with many things, but particularly with Joe. I did not think we would ever have a baby. We had*

*waited too long and did not have much money,
and then suddenly we were given this infant.
Believe me, I could never love anyone more
than I love Joe (although I think I might like him
better when he turns 23!). And loving him, it
was so natural to want to share him back. I'm
just grateful you and your family are such wonderful people—and I particularly appreciate
what Karen told Joe. Please thank her for me.*

*I've always known you could have raised
Joe and he would have been given the love, attention and discipline but I also have seen from
first hand how difficult it is to be a single parent and I applaud you and your family for seeing this.*

*We knew Joe needed to see you if at all pos-
sible because we knew you loved him and he
needed to know that too. And I know he does.*

Love,

Kathy

The Box is full of beautiful letters like this one now. Through good and bad we stayed connected; we communicated. We shared our hopes and fears; we trusted. And in the end, we all made it through. Joe worked through those teenage years and found his place in life, and we were all blessed enough to be a part of it when he did.

When Joe graduated from high school, it was a kind of graduation for us as parents as well. It was a time for all the fears from the past to be blown away like dust as our story came full circle.

Mom, Dad, Rachel, and I drove down in my parents' camper. Steve stayed home with our new baby, Amanda, who was six months old. I usually detest long drives, but being in the camper was much more casual and relaxed, so the time flew as we talked. We were invited to Jerry and Kathy's new house at the lake to spend Saturday afternoon. Sunday morning there was to be a mass for the graduates at their church, then brunch at the restaurant that Joe worked at, followed by the graduation ceremony at his high school, ending the day with a party at their house in town.

We arrived at the lake house at 3:00 p.m. to find that no one was home. We sat on the porch awhile and talked, feeling a bit uncomfortable being there without them. I started to worry that we had gone to the wrong house and that the party was at their old house in town. Kathy had said on the phone that she wasn't sure she'd have the lake house ready in time. They had just bought it a couple weeks ago and hadn't even moved their furniture in yet.

A half hour later, about the time we were going to pack up and head into town, Jerry arrived. He told us that they were still setting up for the party tomorrow at the other house and he hadn't had any time to come out here and clean up. He started frantically working as he talked to us.

Work to be done? Now this was familiar territory. Within moments, Dad was handling a weed whacker, Mom was watering flowers, I was pulling weeds, and Rachel was moving some wood. Working together to

spruce up the yard for the picnic helped to calm some of my fears. It felt good to work instead of worry.

While my family can be laid back when we're having fun, when it comes to work, we get right to it and get it done. It didn't take long at all before the entire yard was cleaned up and ready to go. Jerry was very grateful and couldn't believe we actually finished before anyone arrived.

Kathy and Joe and Joe's girlfriend, Val, all got there just as we finished. It was amazing to me how much Joe had changed over the four years of high school. He went from being short with a bit of a belly to being over six feet tall, very slim, and fit. The biggest surprise was his amazing dark hair that only deepened the Flogel blackness in his eyes. I was very proud to admit that my little baby boy had turned into one very handsome young man. Not only was he extremely good-looking, he was funny and kind and easygoing and had the most compassionate heart I had ever known, next to my dad's. It was no wonder there was a girl hanging tight to his arm!

He gave me a big bear hug, and I teased him about how I couldn't kiss the top of his head the way I usually did. He obliged and bent down. As I always did when seeing him, I just stood looking at him, happy to spend the rest of the day standing right there in the yard. My mom finally broke my spell and butted in for a hug of her own.

The last job on Jerry's list was to put their boat pier back into the water. Mom, Dad, Kathy, Rachel, Val, and I sat on the shore and laughed hysterically at the show that unfolded before us. No one seemed to remember

which piece went where or exactly how they were to be put together. After some hilarious attempts at doing the job while staying dry, Joe dove off the shore into the lake. With some help now in the almost freezing water, the job was finally finished. Everyone thought Joe was crazy for diving into the cold water; I thought he did exactly as his grandfather would have done. Looking at Dad's sparkling eyes, I could see he was thinking the same thing.

As the sun went down that evening, we sat by a fire near the lake and listened to Joe sing and play his guitar. Rachel had stuck close to his side the entire day and was curled up under a blanket near him now, watching him sing with absolute pure adoration. Jerry and Dad chatted quietly nearby, and Mom and I sat near the fire, joining Joe in his song. Hanging out with Joe and his family was as comfortable as going to Grandma's for Thanksgiving. I never wanted the day to end.

Later in the evening, after Joe had gone home to his apartment and we were alone with his parents, his mother got out two huge boxes filled with items from Joe's childhood. Looking through the scrapbooks, seeing his life, his accomplishments, I saw that he had the life I wished for, hoped for, when he was born.

Seeing him with the T-ball team, swim team, peewee football, choir, and band, I knew just how different his life would have been if I had raised him. I never could have involved him in so much. I wouldn't have had the money or time to let him explore all these options. I remembered when he was thirteen and his father told me how they covered the basement walls with egg cartons to

give his band a place to play and record. We wouldn't have had a basement; we would have been lucky to have had a house at all.

I ached to have been the one who was there for him, the one who cheered at his games and cried at his concerts. But I could see it was a fantasy, and reality was that not only were Kathy and Jerry the ones there, but it was because of them that those moments occurred at all. I was filled with gratitude.

The next morning Jerry and Kathy met us in front of their church for the graduation mass. It was a beautiful, large church and filled to its brim. I was completely unprepared for the emotional experience it would present. My chest started to tighten when I knelt to pray before sitting, and I thanked God for allowing me to share this day in Joe's life.

The tightness increased and my breathing quickened when the opening music began. As usual, I had the hymnal open to the appropriate page and was ready to join in the singing. We began, and I looked back down the aisle to see the priest enter, followed by the graduates. I waited, standing next to Jerry and Kathy, and watched as my baby, their son, walked up the aisle. The mass to honor the graduates would last one hour. But for me, it would feel like nine months and three days.

When I saw Joe, dressed up and looking amazingly grown up, everything in my body got tight. I couldn't breathe; I couldn't sing; I couldn't move. What I did do was cry.

The tears came pouring out. At first I didn't even realize it, until my hands that were folded in front of me began to feel wet. I tried desperately to wipe them away, but it was hopeless. All of a sudden I felt as though the only people in the church were Joe and me. With every step forward he took, my mind took a step back. Soon, all I could see was myself, pregnant, standing in the pew knowing it was the last time I would get to attend church because it was too shameful to let anyone find out.

Everything came flooding back. Being scared, being ashamed, being angry. Watching Joe walk to the front of church, in front of a congregation that obviously cared for and loved him, seeing him smile and proudly sit in the front row—it all felt like some kind of contradiction.

Rachel was becoming worried, my crying had escalated into soft sobs, and I couldn't even speak to her. I chided myself for my choice of outfits, even though I had spent a week planning just the right one, because the black pants and white dress shirt had no pockets to speak of, and no place to stuff a tissue. I had none in my purse, and my face was quickly becoming a disaster. As much as I tried I could not stop the flow of tears. No one had a tissue. Dad even had stopped carrying the hankie he always had in his pocket for us when we were little and needed to blow our nose in church.

So I just let the tears fall.

The speaker introduced the graduates from their church, talking about their contributions: in the choir, teaching Sunday School, reader, playing music for mass,

active in the youth group, etc. When she got to Joe, she paused a moment to think, then shrugged and laughed as she said, "Joe, well, he just does everything!" She went on to list some of his many contributions.

This only added to my tears. At first I wasn't even sure why I was crying; it came on so fast and just did not seem to want to let go. My mind was frantically flashing between the past and the present, making me physically dizzy. I had to lean on Rachel in order to stay standing. All of my worries and fears resurfaced, the days spent rocking, rubbing my stomach, and praying, asking God to watch over him and take care of him. The hours spent in my bedroom crying, begging God to help me make the right decision. The years spent praying that I had.

Slowly, my mind started to focus. God had watched over my son. In this church, with these people, God had cared for him and protected him and given him love. The life I had prayed Joe would have was only the beginning. The baby who wasn't allowed to enter my church had been welcomed with open arms into this church and had flourished within its love. It was absolutely overwhelming. I cried so hard I couldn't speak. I wasn't feeling sadness or regret. I was feeling immense relief and peace.

The peace I had felt reading those first letters from Joe's parents was only a heartbeat compared to the peace that enveloped me that day in the church. And I knew. I knew I had made the right choice for me, for my family, and, most important, for Joe. I was overwhelmed with pride. In Joe, for growing up to be such an amazing person. In myself, that I had loved Joe enough to do what

was right. It was not the easy route. I had endured years of questioning my choice and defending my choice to others who questioned it. It was time to give myself a break: I DID do the right thing, and I did it because I loved him. No more questions.

I left that church feeling as though I had just sat down with God himself and had a long heart-to-heart talk. He had listened to my prayers and answered them, even though there had been times I had doubted he was listening. Joseph had the life I had dreamed for him, and more. He was the incredible young man that he was because of the life he had. How could I have ever thought that it should have been different?

As I left the church and entered into the sunlight, Jerry came over and held me. All I could say was, "Thank you."

Surprised by my comment, Jerry looked into my eyes and replied, "No—thank YOU." We stood together crying.

Slowly, we walked back to my parents' camper. Finally, I managed a few words. "If I had known. If I could have seen how wonderful his future was going to be, it would have been so much easier." I broke into more tears.

My mom said firmly, "No, it would not."

I thanked Jerry and Kathy for letting me be a part of this day. In turn, they thanked me for letting them have Joseph. They said he was who he was because of all of us—that the connection to my family and me was too strong to deny and that we had all played a part in the man he now was. There no longer seemed to be a distinc-

tion between Joe's adoptive family and his birth family—we were all just family.

When we finally drove away from the church, Rachel sat near my side, her arm around me, and asked, "Are you okay, Mom?"

I hugged her close, kissing the top of her head, and answered, "Yes."

Joe and I walked together from their house to the restaurant where we were all having brunch together. On the sidewalk outside, he introduced me to some of his friends. It took a moment before it even registered: Joe had introduced me as his birthmother. He had said it so casually and calmly that I didn't even notice it until we turned to walk inside. We hadn't had a chance to discuss this at all. I had no idea how many people knew he was adopted or if anyone knew anything about me at all or knew I was going to be there. Apparently, Joe's parents had taken "openness" to heart because not only did every person we meet know that Joe was adopted, they knew I was his birthmother as well. Everyone around me seemed completely at ease with all of this, but I wasn't sure how to feel. While I had never deliberately hidden it, I hadn't exactly loudly proclaimed my birthmother status over the years.

The old feelings started to creep back. Were they judging me? What were they thinking about me? Were they assuming I didn't want him? Did they think I didn't have any morals, that I wasn't a good person? I watched

everyone in the restaurant, sure that they were all talking about me.

As Joe took me on a tour of the kitchen and office, he introduced me so easily as birthmother that even I began to get comfortable with it. I realized that he was not using the title as a way to make a revelation about his adoption status—everyone already knew. They also obviously knew we had a relationship, so the title did nothing more than place my face in the sea of family faces that abounded that particular day. When Joe used the term, it sounded just as ordinary as saying "aunt" would have, and most of the reactions to it were so welcoming that after awhile I was sure I was the only one who was having a problem with it.

I had always had a problem with the title "birthmother," mostly because, for me, it conjures up an image of giving birth and having someone take the baby away. It also only focuses on that one moment—the birth—that I am entitled to claim. The term completely dismisses the years of love and concern I had felt for Joe, regardless of the fact that he no longer lived with me. But for this one day, hearing Joe use the term with pride, it didn't seem so bad.

At the table, Kathy insisted I sit next to Joe. Her level of unselfishness and her complete trust in our relationship surprised me. I don't know if I had been in her shoes if I would have been able to give up being next to my son at any moment on his graduation day.

Joe began telling animated stories about the restaurant, the people who worked there, and the customers.

He obviously loved every part of it, and at eighteen he was one of their youngest assistant managers. His favorite part of the job was when a customer had a complaint. When a customer was upset about something, he would offer them a free meal or ice cream and suddenly change their mood from sour to thankful. He described it as an unbelievable sense of power to be able to change someone's bad day into a good day. Joe's humanitarian approach to his job amazed me.

At the high school, Jerry and Kathy had saved us seats and put me in between the two of them. The graduates marched in, and I briefly noticed that Joe's shirt collar didn't seem to show above the top of his gown. It wasn't until Joe walked up onto the bleachers facing the audience to perform with the show choir that I noticed there were no pants visible underneath his gown as well.

The school principal began to speak. He congratulated the kids for all their hard work, discussed their unlimited, bright future. Then at the end, he asked the parents responsible for getting them to this point to stand and be recognized. I sat and watched as Kathy and Jerry stood on either side of me. Then, simultaneously, they looked down to me and reached out their hands. Kathy said, "You belong here too," and holding my hands tight, they pulled me up to stand between them.

Again, I cried tears of thankfulness. I just could not imagine this day being any more perfect. Jerry and Kathy were the most understanding, compassionate people I

had ever met. Joe had grown into a wonderful, caring, charismatic, independent, and adventurous young man.

As the graduates filed out of the gym, Joe turned to flash that infectious smile and opened his gown to reveal the red Speedo that had long since replaced his suit and tie. I smiled as I thought, "Yep, he's just like Dad."

Chapter Nine

ADOPTION'S
HAPPY ENDING

doption seems to have been in a constant state of change. Society has been trying to find the right answers, the right approach to an unplanned pregnancy, the right framework for a relationship between adoptive families and birth families. I believe we are getting closer to accepting the truth—that there is no one "right" answer for everyone. But this is always right: a commitment to honesty, respect, and understanding. With these attributes as the cornerstone of an adoption arrangement, what evolves will be right for those whose lives are now and forever connected by the love for a child.

We have come so far in our society. We have learned from the mistakes of the past. We are changing the laws and practices in this field. We are helping those who choose adoption to navigate this new relationship and follow it through without regret.

However, there is more we can do. As we grow into a global society, international adoption has become the new frontier for childless families. While the motives have stayed true—children being adopted out of love—the practices have fallen prey to the myths and misconceptions of the past. While we have changed the practice of closed adoption here in the United States for domestic adoptions, little has been done to improve the practice for international adoption. Closed adoption practices are the standard, and I fear that in the years to come we will be a country filled with adoptees who have been hurt by this practice and feel the need to heal by embarking on difficult, and perhaps futile, searches for their birth families.

Adoptive families have the power to change this outcome. Armed with the knowledge of our past, you are able to elicit change in the industry and help to create laws that will provide your children with the connections they need.

At the very least, adoptive families—whether involved in a closed or open adoption, international or domestic— have the power to teach their children the values of respect, trust, and understanding by being honest with them and respecting their beginnings.

To the girls and women reading this book and facing the decision for adoption, you have the power to create your own happy endings. Be the one to determine your future—and that of your child. Find the answer that is right for both of you. Surround yourself with people who can support you through this journey ahead.

For adoptive parents and birthmothers who have created relationships through adoption, build on the love you have for this child, the love that brought you together. Take a chance and trust one another. Respect one another. Try to understand the other's point of view. Support one another as the child grows older. Be honest.

For adoptees, understand the bravery it took for your birthmother to make the choice she did. Respect the commitment your adoptive parents have made to you. Trust all of them to be honest with you and to do what is best for you.

For all the counselors, friends, and family members of those in the adoption triad, come to truly understand the emotional journey facing them. Respect the fact that this is an immensely personal experience, and take the time to learn their story.

I thank you for hearing mine.

OUR HAPPY ENDING

Adoptees often have questions. Many want to know "why?" Some, like my son when he was younger, just want to get to know their "other mother" and learn where some of their features or talents or mannerisms came from. In open adoption many questions can be answered as they arise, putting fears to rest. Adoptees are assured of their birthmothers' love their entire lives, and the model of respect and understanding that the adoptive parents provide the child through their open arrange-

ment with the birthmother lays a foundation of peace for the child regarding her status as an adoptee.

My son has this sense of peace. I credit his adoptive parents for this. When we did meet for the first time, he had no sense of anger or bitterness. There was no confusion or pain. He simply missed me. In the years after this our relationship built slowly, always looking ahead and never behind. Each year I wondered if the time had come when he would ask for answers, and each year passed uneventfully. We took the time to get to know each other, to share the stories of our present and our dreams for the future, and we left the past alone.

When I began to write our story, I knew I couldn't share it with others until I had shared it with him. I met him at my parents' campground and stole him away to the house, where we could be alone and talk. I told him what I was writing and that it was the story he had never asked me to share with him. I asked if he would like to hear it, and I offered to throw it out and leave it be if that's what he wanted. He admitted that he had wondered what had happened, why I had chosen adoption, but said that he had never wanted to upset me by asking, so he had let it go. Just like Dad all those years ago, Joe had put aside what he had needed out of concern for me. This connection brought me to tears.

I held his hands and told him he had every right to ask any question he wanted to and that I would always be willing to answer. As I do better writing than I do talking, he agreed that I could read to him the first draft of our story that I wrote for this book. We sat side by side

on my parents' couch, holding hands, and I read aloud to him. Together, we laughed, we cried, and while I read the difficult chapter of my three days with him, he put his arm around me to console me. Twenty years earlier I had held him and was strong for him. Now, here he was holding me, offering his strength in return.

After hearing his story, Joe understood why I cried every time I saw him, but he also understood why I had no regrets. He thanked me for giving him the family and the life that he had and for waiting through all those years to be with him again. He told me that he never doubted my love, that it always gave him strength. Then he told me to share our story.

He said he wanted others to understand. Over the years he had encountered many who felt sorry for him that he was adopted, and he never understood why. He loved his family. He knew I loved him, and he had a good life. Why be sorry? He said most people expected him to be angry with me. When he told them he was not and they questioned why, he said his answer was simple: "Because she loves me."

REFERENCES

American Academy of Pediatrics Committee on Adolescence. 1989. "Counseling the Adolescent about Pregnancy Options." *Pediatrics* 83:135–37.

Buckingham, Robert W., and Mary P. Derby. 1997. *I'm Pregnant; Now What Do I Do?* Amherst, N.Y.: Prometheus Books.

Fravel, Deborah Lewis, Ruth G. McRoy, and Harold D. Grotevant, 2000. "Birthmother Perceptions of the Psychologically Present Adopted Child: Adoption Openness and Boundary Ambiguity." *Family Relations* 49:379–87.

Gorle, Rev. Howard R. N.d. "Knowledge of the Grieving Process." http://www.hospicenet.org/html/knowledge.html. Accessed February 6, 2006.

Gross, Harriet. 1993. "Open Adoption: A Research-Based Literature Review and New Data." *Child Welfare* 77:269–84.

Jones, Merry Bloch. 1993. *Birthmothers: Women Who Have Relinquished Babies for Adoption Tell Their Stories.* Chicago: Chicago Review Press.

Moorman, Margaret. *Waiting to Forget.* 1996. New York: Norton.

Pertman, Adam. 2000. *Adoption Nation: How the Adoption Revolution Is Transforming America.* New York:

Basic Books.

Silber, Kathleen, and Phylis Speedlin. 1983. *Dear Birth-mother: Thank You for Our Baby*. San Antonio: Co-rona.

Swanson, Bev. . 2005. *Wide My Ocean, Deep My Grief: A Gentle Guide thru the Uncharted Waters of the Grieving Process*. Victoria, B.C.: Trafford.

Weiss, Ann E. 2001. *Adoptions Today: Questions and Controversies*. Brookfield, Conn.: Twenty-First Century Books.

About the Author

Patricia Dischler is an author who shares her life experiences in order to help others. She lives in Prairie du Sac, Wisconsin, with her husband, Steve, and their two daughters, Rachel and Amanda. From her experience as a birthmother who chose an open adoption for her son in 1985, to her experience in child care, Patricia is dedicated to the well-being of children. It is her hope that her books, lectures, and workshops will enrich the quality of children's lives and relationships by offering guidance to the adults who care for them.

Patricia presents lectures at training events to adoptive parents and birthparents for adoption agencies. She shares her personal story with honesty and emotion to illustrate the beauty of adoption when the elements of trust, respect, and understanding are embraced.

To contact the author and for more information
about her speaking calendar, please visit
www.patriciadischler.com